Understanding Charles Dickens' Great Expectations for GCSE

- ## Gavin's Guide for Edexcel and OCR students for 2018 & 2019

By Gavin Smithers

Another one of **Gavin's Guides** – study books packed with insight. They aim to help you raise your grade!

Understanding Charles Dickens' Great Expectations is a complete study guide and has been written especially for students and teachers who are preparing for GCSE and A-Level in Summer 2018 and 2019.

Series Editor: Gill Chilton

Published by Gavin's Guides

Let's Get Started

You've ordered this Gavin's Guide - and thank you for doing so! Understanding Charles Dickens' Great Expectations has been written especially for students (and their teachers) preparing for English Literature exams in Summer 2018 and 2019. But before you start to read on, let me tell you what's in this guide for you …

Dickens' "Great Expectations" is one of the most colourful and characterful of all 19th century novels. No wonder that it is such a success as a core text for English Literature Exams at both GCSE and A-Level and likely to remain so for some years. It is a rich and intriguing story, masterfully told- part fairy tale, part love story, part detective drama, with elements of the gothic, and a healthy dash of humour.

But – and here is the problem for every student sitting more than one exam this summer – it is a long read. Even at a brisk pace, it is likely to take 30 hours cover to cover. And, at this stage in your exam preparation, that may well be time you just do not have.

This Gavin's Guide isn't a substitute for reading the book. And indeed – plot warning here – I make the assumption right from the start *that you have read the book and therefore know how characters develop, and their final fate.*

However!

This Study Guide is comprehensive and analytical enough to mean that, if you are unable to re-read the original book text, you can still master the plot and – more importantly at exam level – understand both the characters and why the author chose the methods that he did.

I am a private tutor in the Cotswolds, Gloucestershire and this book was initially written for my English Literature students. I wrote it to help them achieve good grades – and an understanding of what this clever, careful writer wanted to say. Now, in e-book form or paperback, I hope it may help you too.

What this guide can do

This interpretative guide is intended as a supplement to, not a substitute for, teaching in a school. It has been written especially to help students taking GCSE and A- level exams in Summer 2018 and 2019.

In the exam, students will face the task of writing a 40-minute or a 60-minute essay, depending on the choice of exam board and whether the exam is for GCSE or A – level. This Gavin's Guide aims to help you perform that task wonderfully well.

- Through a breakdown of what happens in each chapter, you will understand the flow of the plot.

- By discovering characters' true (if changing) motivations, you will be able to answer questions about them with confidence.

- As you see, in this guide, how good use of quotations defines and strengthens an argument, you will become confident about using the text under exam conditions to strengthen your argument.

- Sections on popular themes and essay technique will prepare you for a range of questions.

A Gavin's Guide is different from other study guides, as each one is written as if a personal tutor were guiding you, the individual with the exam ahead, to outperform your expectations.

To follow that through, I also offer a valuable extra, at no charge, to readers. If you feel there is something you still don't understand about the text of "Great Expectations", email me direct – at grnsmithers@hotmail.co.uk. I hope to help you further, or point you to further useful resources.

My love of literature began when I studied for an English degree at Oxford. Today, unravelling and appreciating language remains a lifelong passion. If this book can move you towards that too – then it will be doubly worthwhile!

Interested? All you need is a few clear hours … and a willingness to begin with an open, curious mind.

Looking ahead to your Exam Day – and how this book can help

So what sort of a question can you expect?

The examiners will not set a trick question; but it will test your response to a character, ask you to explain what Dickens gains from one of his major themes, or invite you to explain how the narrative is managed in a particular chapter.

Any of these questions is fair. What they really seek to detect is a personal response from you, the student, which shows that you understand the structure of the novel, the key characteristics of Dickens' style, and what Dickens wants to say to us.

Questions about characters give you the opportunity to discuss how Dickens presents them; only Pip and (to a lesser extent) Estella change and develop, although Magwitch's true character only emerges over the last third of the novel, so there is development (and increasing understanding) there too.

The other characters behave consistently throughout, and so we have to be clear about what they contribute to the novel, or what would be lost if any of them were missing.

Neither students nor teachers will have the time to read the novel over and over again. My estimate is that reading Great Expectations cover to cover and at a fairly brisk pace still takes 30 hours. That's a whole school week of lessons – and no doubt you have other subjects and other demands too. But to do well in your exam you DO need to multiple read the book - a single reading is unlikely to enable you to locate and remember key episodes clearly and quickly. So this is where this Gavin's Guide steps in.

I have summarised each chapter, and included an analysis of what is notable in it, not just in terms of the narrative, but with emphasis, too, on Dickens' methods.

To read a Gavin's Guide you simply need a few clear hours (not 30!) and an open, curious mind. You will find key quotations used as evidence for the analysis. The chapter by chapter analysis is intended as a reference point- whether you are a student or a teacher, it should help you to focus on key chapters and on what is important in them.

The idea here is that, **if you are preparing to write an essay, or if you are researching a character because you are expecting a question about them, you can use the analysis in this guide, alongside your knowledge and prior reading of the text, to highlight a number of key points.**

This will make your revision and study much quicker, and more productive, than it would be if you were using the novel itself on its own.

I have also included a short analysis of how the action develops over groups of chapters in order to clarify the structure of the narrative.

At the end of each of Dickens' original three volumes (that's at the end of chapter 19, the end of chapter 39, and at the end of the novel) you will find a short note of the cast of characters and locations for each of the chapters you've been reading in that third of the novel.

If you are looking for a scene, or tracking the appearances of any of the characters, you can save time by referring to these lists.

All of this material so far also lends itself to use in the classroom, as the basis of a discussion of any part of the text of the novel. My intention is for it to be of practical help to teachers as well as students.

Finally, there is the question of how to write an essay for an exam. I've provided two sample questions and answers. The answers aren't intended to be a substitute for students' own ideas; far from it. But I have included them in order to provide a template for organising material and structuring an essay. You will see that, if you use the cast and locations lists, and then use the chapter analyses, you will be able to find material and ideas quickly and easily. This leaves you more time to construct and develop your argument.

"Great Expectations" is a long read. At first sight, it seems sprawling- George Orwell criticised Dickens for accumulating unnecessary detail.

But none of the detail is unnecessary. *One of the main findings in this guide is that there are connections- often many chapters apart- which cement the edifice of the novel together. Once you see them, it is my belief that your admiration for Dickens, and for his command of the detail of his plot, will be all the greater.*

Students who are reading for an exam- and their teachers- are in a difficult position, because Dickens repays time spent re-reading him; time you may not have. Particularly when it comes to revising, you may have to choose some chapters over others to re-read and analyse, because it may be unrealistic to read the whole work again.

I have provided a detailed analysis of the action of each chapter, and, at the same time, an analysis of the technical and broader issues we find there. I've chosen to do both of these things in the same place for each chapter because I believe that is the most helpful way to show you how the novel is constructed. This means **that some chapters receive detailed and extended attention. It also means that you should read the whole of this guide.** Take your time, go at your own pace – and I wish you every success in your studies.

Why Great Expectations is such a Great Novel

The novel is, first and foremost, an intriguing, and sometimes exciting, story. It combines elements of the fairy tale, the quest, the growing up tale, the Prodigal Son, the gothic horror story, the ghost story, the romance, the mystery, the detective story…………all in a way we recognise, yet find fresh.

It reflects Dickens' many interests, too- namely the way criminal law works, and the death penalty; the greatness and greed of London, as seen by its insiders and outsiders; his own infatuation (with an actress, Ellen Terney) and his guilt over his lack of feeling for his "dull" wife Kate. There is also space for his intense interest in intra-family relationships; his pain over debt and financial exploitation; his love of the arts, public performance and the theatre; and, finally, his musings on what constitutes gentility, and on how helping others helps (or does not really help) both us and them.

Dickens' plot depends greatly on coincidence- something which modern literary theory says the serious novel is supposed to avoid, because it sacrifices credibility. Dickens, though, gets away with it; just as he gets away with most things (though, if you read this guide closely, you can see whether you agree with me on where the slight weaknesses lie). The novel teems with life; it rarely, if ever flags. It isn't high-brow but it isn't simplistic. It has some characters we don't much like, but many of them- especially Biddy, Joe and Pip himself-we come to care about, deeply.

<u>I suspect that if we could interview Dickens, he would say that his novel is less about "great expectations" than about human nature; about loyalty; about love, of various kinds, and how you measure it.</u>

For this reason, I find it dangerous to simplify this complex narrative as a morality tale of sin and atonement. It does not have a strong or explicit **moral** purpose, except in its sympathy for the condemned "criminal". You will find a number of themes which run through the novel, and come out via Pip's narrative voice; they are not what the novel is about, but they are a way of unifying the narrative.

That narrative is really about how a boy becomes a man; or, by extension, about **what we need to learn before we can take our rightful place in the adult world.**

Chapter by Chapter analysis of "Great Expectations"

Dickens' novel was first published in three parts in 1861. It has 59 chapters; 19 chapters form the first part; chapters 20-39 make up part two; and chapters 40-59 are part three.

Book One (of three)

Chapter 1

Dickens introduces us to Pip (aged about seven) and gives us his first terrifying (but also comical) encounter with the escaped convict who, we will learn, much later, is Magwitch. Just as Magwitch's identity as Pip's benefactor is a secret for most of the novel (it is only revealed in chapter 39), his actual identity is secret here.

Pip Pirrip is a palindromic name; (the dictionary definition of palindromic is a word that reads the same backwards as forwards). Perhaps there is a hint here that **Pip will** somehow **end up in a position similar to where he starts from.**

The second paragraph of the novel establishes that Pip is an orphan; his parents were Philip, and "also Georgiana wife of the above". There is a note of pathos in the fact that he has no idea of what they looked like, and that Pip's "five little brothers" had died in infancy too. As he looks at his family's graves, he is starting to cry, and is "the small bundle of shivers growing afraid of it all"- of the disadvantages and hopelessness of his own situation. He describes himself as "undersized….and not strong".

It is worth noting that Pip associates with their premature deaths the idea that they "gave up trying to get a living, exceedingly early in that universal struggle"; this is a clue that **the novel will be dominated by the struggles of various people to survive financially in a harsh world. Pip and Magwitch both go from poverty to wealth and back again**. The characters in the novel will fall into three categories- the criminal class, the working class and the moneyed class- and it will explore the similarities and differences between them.

Dickens takes time to construct the landscape, not just of the churchyard, which is "bleak" and "overgrown with nettles", but of the threatening and dangerous area beyond it; "the dark flat wilderness" of the marshes, which stretches to the sea twenty miles away, is "leaden", "savage", and the sky is "a row of long angry red lines and dense black lines". The marshes are sodden by the river and the tide and the rain, and the image at the end of the chapter is of **the gibbet, in the distance**, with chains on it**; Pip imagines that Magwitch is the pirate who was executed there**, "come to life", and that, in the graveyard, he is "eluding the hands of the dead people" who are trying to pull him underground. **The threat of Magwitch being hanged dominates the latter part of the novel.**

Magwitch is "a fearful man" with a "terrible voice" and "an old rag tied round his head". He threatens to allow his shadowy and violent companion (whose identity we do not know, but who is Compeyson) to cut Pip's throat, and to cut out his heart and liver and roast and eat them, if Pip reveals their meeting here. He makes Pip take an oath that he will bring him food and a file in the morning- just as he carries a Bible on which he makes people swear their commitments later.

Magwitch describes himself as an "Angel" compared with Compeyson; later, we understand why this is true (Compeyson dominates, exploits and abuses Old 'Orlick just as he had done Magwitch, for his own greedy purposes). Magwitch describes the stealth and inevitability with which Compeyson tracks his victims- "a boy…may think himself comfortable and safe, but (Compeyson) will softly creep and creep his way to him and tear him open". This **is prophetic of the way in which Compeyson organises the recapture and condemnation of Magwitch in chapters 54 and 56.**

But there is humour in the scene; the visual humour of Magwitch turning Pip upside down so that he can empty his pockets, and so that Pip sees the church upside down; and the misunderstanding that when Pip says his mother is in the graveyard, "there", Magwitch thinks she is alive. Pip refers to her as the inscription on her tombstone indicates- not "Georgiana", but "Also Georgiana".

Magwitch mispronounces "point" as "pint", "victuals" (food) as "wittles", "very" as "wery", and "in vain" as "in wain". He has a dialect; he says "alonger" instead of "along with", "lookee" instead of "look ye", "hid" for "hidden", "undertook" for "undertaken", "a" for "an", "ain't" for "am not", "pecooliar" for "peculiar" . His grammar is imprecise- "them wittles". He conveniently asks Pip who he lives with, which allows us to understand, for the second time, that Pip lives with his older sister "Mrs Joe", who is married to Joe Gargery, the blacksmith. Magwitch needs a blacksmith's file, to release his prisoner's leg irons.

The way he speaks indicates that Magwitch is uneducated (like Joe) and deprived of opportunity; the uneducated tend to be looked down on in this novel. His violence is enough to frighten Pip into obeying him, but it has something of the pantomime villain in it; he calls Pip "you little devil" and "you young dog", but the threat of cannibalism is not his own- it is his companion's, and so one step removed. **Magwitch is already protecting Pip**, and he only wants the bare minimum to enable him to survive his immediate, desperate crisis of imminent starvation and immobility.

Magwitch has no intention of hurting Pip; he frightens him only by "tilting" him. But the image which stays with us is of the gibbet, and Pip seems to have an intuition that Magwitch, though not a dead man walking, is a man whose life is under threat.

Just as Pip is a "small bundle of shivers", the convict is "shuddering". It may be from fear or it may be from extreme cold, but **they are linked in their discomfort**. When Magwitch tilts Pip on the gravestone, "his eyes looked most powerfully down into mine, and mine looked most helplessly up into his", and, out of fear, Pip "clung to him with both hands". When he is dying in hospital, in chapter 56, Magwitch has no power in his eyes, and he wants Pip to rest his hands on his. They are still connected intimately, even after Pip knows that Magwitch's fortune has been lost, but it is now Pip who is the adult, and Magwitch who is the helpless child.

Chapter 2

Pip goes home to plan how he will take the food he has promised Magwitch. It is Christmas Eve. Pip's sister Mrs Joe is presented to us as a comical character; like Magwitch, she uses violence and the threat of violence to maintain order and secure co-operation. There is verbal humour, when Joe mouths to Pip the word "hulks" and Pip thinks he means "sulks", and visual humour, when Pip hides his bread down the leg of his trousers, and is given a dose of tar-water, because she thinks he has been bolting his food.

Joe's position is comical but uncomfortable; although he is married to Pip's sister, she treats him rather like she treats Pip (as a small boy) - "by hand"- and she uses a "wax-ended piece of cane" called Tickler to enforce domestic discipline. Joe describes her violent temper as the "Ram-page"; she bangs Joe's head against the wall, and she throws Pip at Joe like "a connubial missile". Joe thinks of her outbursts of temper as "squally times".

Mrs Joe is more than twenty years older than Pip, "hard", with "black hair and eyes", and such red skin that Pip thinks she washes herself, not with soap, but with a nutmeg-grater- this represents her abrasive character in her physical appearance. She is "tall and bony", and, unless there are visitors, she is never polite.

She is completely in control of the running of the (wooden) house they live in, and she wears an apron almost all the time, to signify that. Her domestic, "all-powerful" tyranny makes Pip's promise to Magwitch into "a dreadful pledge......a larceny". When Pip asks what a convict is, and what the Hulks (prison-ships) are, her explanation- that robbers are sent there- heightens his sense that he is "going to rob Mrs Joe".

Joe has fair curly hair, a smooth face, and watery eyes. Dickens defines his character unambiguously-

"He was a mild, good-natured, sweet-tempered, easy-going, foolish, dear fellow- a sort of Hercules in strength, and also in weakness". He has no malice in him, and Pip regards him "as a larger species of child, and as no more than my equal". Mrs Joe speaks to him insultingly, and calls him "you staring great stuck pig". Her indiscriminately bad behaviour gives Joe and Pip "freemasonry as fellow-sufferers".

Joe calls Pip "old chap"; Mrs Joe calls him "you young monkey".

Neither of the Gargerys is educated; Joe says "sot" instead of "sat", "is" for "are", "'elth" for "health", "oncommon" for "uncommon", "ain't" for "aren't", "conwict" for "convict", and Mrs Joe uses "was" for "were", "warn't" for "wasn't", "worrit" for "worry". Pip the narrator presents himself as a child who speaks politely and without any dialect or accent.

Dickens undermines the comic tone in the extended scene he creates, with Mrs Joe holding Pip's head under her arm and forcing him to drink a pint of tar-water, by having the noise of the wind from the marshes remind Pip (in the manner of a ghost story) of Magwitch's voice and his threats. He hears the cannon-fire which warns that a second convict has escaped.

The fourth paragraph from the end of the chapter stresses the "mortal" terror Pip feels, by repeating the word "terror" six times. Again, Pip thinks or dreams of the gibbet and the ghostly pirate in his imagination. At the crack of dawn, he hurriedly takes what food he can, including "a beautiful round compact pork pie" which is hidden in a dish on the corner of a high shelf.

We understand why Pip is forced to assist Magwitch (he knows that Pip lives at the blacksmith's) and why he cannot confide in his family (he is terrified of his sister). The chapter ends with Pip running back to the marshes, afraid, just as the first chapter had ended with him running home from the marshes, afraid. He uses the word "larceny" more than once in this chapter, to describe what he sees as his theft from Mrs Joe (can we rob our own home?). He does not make any distinction between the convicts on the Hulks, who Mrs Joe says, "murder, and….rob, and forge, and do all sorts of bad", and himself; although taking what he does to give it to Magwitch is done under the threat of violence and terror. Although Pip is not a criminal, this is how criminals are made. Magwitch himself had been made into a criminal by Compeyson, who had power over him because he could terrorise Magwitch with a secret of his own.

Pip tends to see himself as a criminal because adults are always telling him he is bad. His journey through the novel will teach him that good and bad are relative, and that people who do "bad" things often have good reason- just like this case of his own, where he is "stealing" in order to make another outcast slightly more comfortable.

Chapter 3

Pip returns to the marshes, early on Christmas Day, to keep his promise to Magwitch, but he meets the other convict (not yet identified, but Compeyson).

Pip's anxiety is comic; he thinks of himself as "a boy with somebody else's pork pie", and he defends himself in words to an ox which he feels is looking at him in an accusing way.

The second convict is wearing a leg iron and a hat. He says nothing to Pip, but aims a weak blow at him and runs off. When Pip tells Magwitch he has seen him, Magwitch's hostility to his fellow escaper is clear; Pip leaves him frantically trying to file the iron off his leg so that he can pursue Compeyson.

Magwitch's accent is softer in this chapter (see the changes in words like arterwards, warmint) and his tone to Pip is warmer and less intimidating. Dickens takes care to describe how he eats, like a dog, savagely; how he is haunted by the imagined sounds of soldiers searching for him throughout the night; and he gives him the distinctive click in his throat, "as if he had works in him like a clock, and was going to strike"- this becomes one of the clues to his identity when he comes to see Pip and reveal his patronage later.

This chapter gives Magwitch this identifying mark, and sets up his enmity with Compeyson, without explaining its origins or its significance. This, along with Dickens' secrecy over Magwitch's name and history, creates a sense of mystery and suspense. **The violent and desperate chase here- of Compeyson by Magwitch- is reversed in the final part of the novel.**

Pip is, again, noticeably polite in his speech (which, unlike the Gargerys', is already in standard English); amusingly, he seeks to avoid hurting Magwitch's feelings by not referring directly to leg irons ("the same reason for wanting to borrow a file"). As a small and powerless boy, he is used to people taking offence at him, even where none is intended.

It is an odd start to a Christmas Day. But his convict turns out to be an odd sort of Christmas present, sixteen or seventeen years later.

Chapter 4

Dickens makes the most of the Christmas scene at the Gargerys', with an amusing show of how adults patronise children. We have our first sight of the self-dramatising Mr Wopsle (the church clerk), the ridiculous Pumblechook (Joe's uncle, the reasonably prosperous corn-seller) and the slightly sinister Mr (the wheelwright) and Mrs Hubble. Pip is acutely uncomfortable, and he holds on to the table leg, thinking that his "theft" of the brandy and the pork pie are about to be discovered. Dickens handles the suspense here cleverly.

At the end of the chapter, soldiers appear at the door, with handcuffs; Pip, with the logic and fear of a small child, thinks they are for him, but we know that they cannot be, because he would not be arrested for what he took to Magwitch (and anyway Mrs Joe is still unaware that anything is missing).

Each of these comical characters has a defining physical characteristic. Wopsle has "a Roman nose and large shining bald forehead", and a deep voice and a liking for all things theatrical. Pumblechook is "a large hard-breathing middle-aged slow man, with a mouth like a fish, dull staring eyes, and sandy hair standing upright". Mrs Hubble is "a little curly sharp-edged person in sky-blue". Her husband is "a tough high-shouldered stooping old man" with a bow-legged walk.

The description of Mrs Hubble has some interesting extra detail; she had married a man much older than herself, and so "held a conventionally juvenile position". She, Mrs Joe, Estella, Sarah Pocket, Clara Barley and Biddy all have conventional domestic or family responsibilities which tie them to home and restrict their ability to engage with the wider world; only Miss Skiffins is an exception to the rule.

The subversive boyish signalling between Pip and Joe continues; in the previous chapter they compared the way they ate their bread, and Joe mimed words to Pip; now we find that they have a secret sign- crossing their fingers- to show that Mrs Joe is tetchy. When Pip is being demonised unfairly, Joe demonstrates his support by giving him more and more gravy- so, here, "Joe gave me some more gravy……….Joe gave me some more gravy…….Joe offered me more gravy, which I was afraid to take". The repetition is humorous, but Pip, squeezed into a corner, with Pumblechook's elbow in his face, and the least edible bits of pork to eat, feels goaded like "an unfortunate little bull in a Spanish arena".

As the narrator, Pip recalls that his sister's housekeeping was so meticulous that it was "more uncomfortable…….than dirt itself". She claims he is a "squeaker", and (encouraged by Mrs Hubble) recites the "trouble" he has been, his past illnesses and injuries. The adults look at Pip "with indignation and abhorrence"; we feel sorry for him because he is even less powerful than Joe.

During the Christmas meal, Pip is not allowed to speak; he is seated uncomfortably, and squashed in; he is given the worst of the meat; and he is made the object of the adults' "moral goads", and told to "be grateful". It is hard to see how being lectured and criticised for being "naturally wicious"- purely because he is a child- equates to "enjoying himself with his elders and betters, and improving himself with their conversation". *The point about these adults, and this village, is that there is no possibility of self-improvement.*

Wopsle and Pumblechook are equally pompous, each in their own way. Wopsle thinks he could deliver a better Christmas sermon than the parson, and he picks up Pumblechook's strange idea of "pork", to infer that the young in general, and Pip in particular, are swine, and potentially gluttonous; swine, who live a short life and are not "brought up by hand" (surely there is a literary nod here to Swift's great satire, "A modest proposal", about controlling the population by cooking and eating the children of poor Catholic families).

Pumblechook, at least, is deflated when he drinks what the adults think is brandy, but is tar-water, with which Pip had replaced the brandy he took for Magwitch. The description of him rushing outside and "making the most hideous faces" is a moment of visual comedy. Mrs Joe has "begun to be alarmingly meditative" because she cannot understand how tar has got into the brandy bottle.

Dickens cleverly links together Mrs Joe's general attitude towards Pip (as though he were a "young offender") with his specific "terrors...remorse....wicked secret". The secret- that the pork pie is missing- becomes a source of acute dramatic tension in the closing three paragraphs of the chapter. Dickens slows the action down, to match Pip's helpless fear; when he runs to the door, to escape, he is met- with marvellous timing- by the group of armed soldiers with the handcuffs.

Chapter 5

We return to the marshes with the soldiers who are searching for the two convicts; Pip, as the narrator of the novel, has to be a witness, and Joe and Mr Wopsle take him. Christmas Day, for Magwitch and Compeyson, is anything but comfortable; they are fighting out their hatred of each other, and it is their angry shouts at each other which allow the soldiers to find them.

The soldiers have come to requisition Joe's services as a blacksmith, to mend the broken handcuffs. Their sergeant drinks Pumblechook's wine, and Pumblechook is rather pathetic in the way he takes back the drinks he had given Mrs Joe, to entertain and please the soldiers. He exhibits a false jollity; he has "a fat sort of laugh" because his character is flabby.

The manhunt for the convicts could have been a threatening, dramatic episode, but it is a peaceful pursuit; the two men are apprehended without a struggle, or any sense that they might evade capture, or be shot. The sergeant's prediction that "they'll find themselves trapped in a circle….sooner than they count on" proves true.

The chapter opens with Mrs Joe realising that the pork pie is missing, and it ends with **Magwitch taking responsibility** for its disappearance- he claims that he stole it from the house himself, in order to remove suspicion from Pip. **Magwitch's morality is striking- he is concerned that Pip's help should not expose him to punishment.**

For Pip, the still unidentified Magwitch is "my fugitive friend on the marshes"; the prospect of his being captured is a kind of Christmas entertainment for the soldiers and the others, who refer to the escaped convicts as "the two **villains**". Pip, by contrast, thinks of them as "**poor wretches**" and confides to Joe that he hopes the search is unsuccessful. Joe agrees; his view is that, whatever crime a man may have committed, he is a "**poor miserable fellow-creatur**", and should not starve to death as a consequence. The saying is that there is no honour among thieves, but **there is compassion among underdogs (like Pip and Joe) for fellow underdogs like Magwitch.**

Pip worries, naturally, that Magwitch ("my convict") will think that he has broken his promise of secrecy, and has brought the soldiers, having betrayed Magwitch. After Magwitch is rearrested, Pip does not speak to him, but tries to convey his loyalty with a hand movement and a shake of his head. Magwitch, very attentive, "gave me a look that I did not understand". He does not look at Pip again, but becomes thoughtful; confesses to the sergeant that he took the food, including the pie, and apologises to Joe for it. This is a striking proof that Magwitch is decent and honourable, and that he repays Pip's good deed to him with care. From the point of view of managing the narrative, it prevents future awkwardness between Mrs Joe and Joe and Pip, because the disappearance of the food now has a proper explanation.

The sergeant finds Magwitch and Compeyson fighting in a ditch. Magwitch derives satisfaction from handing Compeyson in. Compeyson, who has had the worse of the fight, claims that Magwitch tried to kill him. Magwitch tells the sergeant that he was determined not to let the other man "make a tool of me afresh and again"- another unexplained reference (later, we learn that Compeyson had exploited Magwitch, as he goes on to do to Orlick). Compeyson is frightened of Magwitch, and cannot look at him directly. Magwitch says it was the same "when we were tried together". We have to wait until chapter 42 (sixteen years later) to find out what this means- Magwitch explains then how **Compeyson was imprisoned for seven years, as opposed to his own sentence of 14, because the jury perceived him as a "gentleman".** Magwitch has been seeking revenge ever since. Here, he tells the sergeant , "He's a gentleman, if you please, this villain. Now, the Hulks has got its gentleman again, through me." He says that he has sacrificed his own opportunity to escape in order to drag Compeyson back into captivity.

The lame and limping convicts are taken under armed guard to the boat which returns them to the prison ship moored offshore. At the landing-place, there is a wooden hut which smells of tobacco and whitewash, and has "a low wooden bedstead, like an overgrown mangle without the machinery". This seems an irrelevant detail, but Dickens uses individual objects to create a sense of place. There is more detailed description of the inside of the sluice-house, where Pip is nearly killed, in Chapter 53; and, when we think of the Gargerys' house, we think of Mrs Joe's four matching "little white crockery poodles on the mantelshelf, each with a black nose and a basket of flowers in his mouth" (Chapter 4).This last piece of decoration finds its own echo in Chapter 57, when Joe tells Pip that when Orlick robbed Pumblechook, "they stuffed his mouth full of flowering annuals to prevent his crying out".

Summary - Chapters 1-5

With the recapture of Magwitch, a small incident in Pip's life, which has taken place over 24 hours on Christmas Eve and Christmas Day, appears to be over and done with. We might think this is a false start to the novel, because it does not appear to be leading to anything significant; **the meaning and importance of the episode is a mystery.**

It is a mystery because Dickens keeps Magwitch's identity from Pip and from us. But, in the honourable way Magwitch deals with Pip, and the unspeaking glance, the relationship between them which is to be so pivotal is established. It is only when we return to the beginning of the novel, asking ourselves "how the Dickens did Dickens manage that?", that we can find these significant details, and see how and where the seeds of the later action are sown.

It is not only the convicts who have no name we can use to refer to them; Pip's older sister, Mrs Joe, has no name of her own. She is a caricature, always behaving in a consistent way, with harshness, and a show of resenting Pip and the "trouble" he causes her.

We can already begin to draw a distinction between **Dickens' comic characters and his serious ones. The serious ones- Pip, Joe and Magwitch- have more depth and character, and there is more variety in what they say. They speak more intelligently and sensibly, and they are good at expressing their thoughts. The comic characters- Mrs Joe, Pumblechook, Wopsle- are one-dimensional, almost cartoonish, and we empathise with them less**.

They soon have the capacity to frustrate us, because their behaviour is simplistic. They are *childish* and rather bad-natured; whereas the serious characters- Pip, Joe, Magwitch- are *childlike* in their fundamental good nature.

It is a useful rule to remember that Dickens' characters fall into two groups- those who patronise and look down on others, and those who do not. Those who do not- Pip (eventually), Joe, Magwitch, Wemmick- see the good in others, are comfortable with their place in the world, do not resent the difficulties in their lives, and have liberal attitudes; those who do patronise others tend to be critical, blind to their own faults, and resentful, because they feel that other people never give them their due. Pumblechook keeps appearing in this way.

A Task for students

See if you can identify and list the small details in these opening chapters which help to define the overall tone of the novel.

I would choose the comment about Pip's five dead brothers giving up the struggle to earn a living; the gloomy presence on the marshes of the gibbet and the chains; the poverty Pip lives in, with his controlled allowances of bread, water and milk (rather like a prison); Magwitch's dignity in the face of his own struggle to survive.

At this stage, we cannot, as readers, say precisely, in one sentence, what the novel will be about; but we feel that Pip deserves better than to be ignored or insulted over Christmas dinner by the adults, and attacked by Mrs Joe with "Tickler". Pip has an essential goodness and dignity which mean that he deserves a better life than the one he has been born into, as an orphan in a small wooden house near the dank, dismal marshes, in outlaw country.

Chapter 6

Pip is put to bed after the adults have speculated on how Magwitch broke into the house- Pumblechook's ridiculous idea that he had come down the chimney (like Santa Claus?!) is accepted because none of the other adults has an alternative explanation.

Pip could explain it, of course, but he feels disinclined to tell Mrs Joe; and he is afraid to tell Joe what really happened, in case it affects Joe's opinion of him, and Joe thinks of him as someone who interferes with the kitchen supplies. Pip cannot resolve his "cowardly" feelings, and has not yet seen people doing so in the wider world. So he decides to say nothing more to Joe about the fact that his connection with Magwitch is personal, arising from their meeting in Chapter 1.

Looking back, Pip sees this as a formative experience. Having "been too cowardly to avoid doing what I knew to be wrong"- although it is hard to see how he could have avoided aiding and abetting Magwitch- he is now "too cowardly to do what I knew to be right", and so fails to disclose the whole truth to Joe. Because he has no role-model- no father, or other sensible adult he can rely on- he does not know what to do, and fears for Joe's opinion of him.

Chapter 7

It is about a year later, in the winter again. Mrs Joe has gone out on a periodic trip with Pumblechook, who, as a middle-aged bachelor, needs her help when he does his shopping on market-day.

Pip reflects on his situation at the time; he could barely read, and habitually misunderstood the simple formulaic language of the church. He expects, when he is older, to become Joe's apprentice, and, meanwhile, he is farmed out to do any small casual jobs such as scaring birds or picking up stones.

Pip attends Mr Wopsle's great-aunt's evening school (she charges two pence a week), which is so disorganised that it is virtually useless; Biddy (the great-aunt's granddaughter) runs the shop in the same room.

Dickens introduces Biddy to us in her absence; like Pip, she is an orphan who has been "brought up by hand"; she is always dirty, dishevelled and poorly shod. She helps Pip in his struggles with the alphabet and with numbers.

Most of this chapter is used to explain how poor Pip's prospects are, and to show us why Joe puts up with the domestic tyranny and violence Mrs Joe inflicts on them both. Joe lived here with his own parents; his father was a blacksmith, but also a violent alcoholic, from whom his mother ran away several times, taking Joe with her. But she was always forced to go back, so Joe could never have any coherent education.

Although he does not admit it, he can only read two letters, "j" and "o". After his parents died, in quick succession, Joe was lonely, and he met and married Pip's sister, and insisted that she brought Pip with her. She is hostile to the idea of any education for Joe, because it might undermine her power of controlling him; her view is that an educated Joe "might rise. Like a sort of rebel".

Joe is willing to tolerate her violent behaviour because, having seen his own mother suffer so much at the hands of his father, he is "dead afeerd of going wrong in the way of not doing what's right by a woman". He is prepared to avoid conflict, be submissive, and work hard, as a reaction to his own experience as a child. He aspires to at least some education and literacy, but tells Pip that they must help each other on this "on the sly". His submissiveness takes the form of a physical gesture- "he drew the back of his hand across his nose with his usual conciliatory air"- whenever Mrs Joe is angry, which is most of the time.

What we might be inclined to see as a weakness in Joe- a willingness to be bullied-stems from his not caring if he is "a little ill-conwenienced myself" (i.e. beaten by his wife). Even in spite of his father's faults, Joe had wanted to give his tombstone the inscription

Whatsume'er the failings on his part/ Remember reader he were that good in his hart

Similarly, although he concedes that Mrs Joe is "the Mogul…heavy…on the Rampage….a Buster", he insists that she "is a fine figure of a woman". **His loyalty is absolute**, regardless of "the world's opinions". He regards himself and Pip as "ever the best of friends", and after Joe has explained his values to Pip here, Pip develops "a new admiration of Joe.....a new sensation of feeling conscious that I was looking up to Joe in my heart". Pip comes to admire Joe's loyalty more and more, but, in the way he fails to assert himself, Joe is weak, and a poor example for Pip to follow in his dealings with Miss Havisham and Estella.

The explanation Joe gives for his own apparent weakness helps us to understand him better. But the way in which he allows his wife to steamroller him is a poor model for Pip to build his own relationships with women on. Moreover, when Joe, goaded by his wife's manufactured sense that her honour has been offended, picks a fight with Orlick in Chapter 15, it has tragic repercussions- Orlick avenges himself with the attack which condemns her to being an invalid and to an early death. <u>In Joe's idealistic subservience to women- he puts them on a pedestal and allows them to mistreat him- there is a foreshadowing of Pip's future difficulty with Estella.</u>

In trying to make amends for the adult wrongs he saw in his own childhood, Joe allows his wife to bully him. Both Miss Havisham's coldness towards men and Magwitch's generosity (having lost his own family, as far as he knows) are miscalculated responses to events in their own lives, which have bad consequences for others. **Like Joe with Mrs Joe, Pip is too submissive to Estella and Miss Havisham** for his own good. The problem with seeing no evil (like Joe) and giving other people the benefit of the doubt- assuming that they are "good in their hart"- is that it denies us the ability to make judgments which is so necessary in the grown up world. Joe does not care what Magwitch may or may not have done; he excuses all manner of violence or cruelty. Estella cannot grow up until she challenges and rejects Miss Havisham's misguided, obsessive vengeance, and Pip can only grow up once he realises the value of loyalty and goodness for their own sake.

The last part of the chapter sets up the next mystery. Mr Pumblechook is a tenant of Miss Havisham, whose reputation "for miles around" is "as an immensely rich and grim lady who lived in a large and dismal house barricaded against robbers, and who led a life of seclusion".

Astonishingly, Mrs Joe announces that Miss Havisham "wants this boy to go and play there"; she gives Pip no choice. Pumblechook, Joe's uncle, thinks that "this boy's fortune may be made by his going to Miss Havisham's", and so he has offered to take him home with him that evening, so that he can personally deliver Pip to her in the morning. Pip thus leaves for his first night away from Joe, and with Miss Havisham's motive a complete mystery.

Mrs Joe regards the invitation rather as we might regard a lottery ticket. There is nothing to be lost, and, she thinks, much to be gained- despite the fact that Joe, Pip and Mrs Joe herself are completely unknown to Miss Havisham. Mrs Joe and Pumblechook have already developed great expectations of a connection which has not yet even begun.

Chapter 8

This, like Chapter 7, is a longer episode in which we have a mixture of action, in the second part of the chapter, and description or deepening of character and atmosphere in the first; plus some humour at the expense of Pumblechook. We see Satis House and Miss Havisham, for the first time, as Pip sees them. There is an atmosphere of the Gothic, if not the horror film, here; **just as the gibbet of the marshes haunts Pip's imagination, and casts the threat of death by hanging over Magwitch, so Miss Havisham seems barely alive, a character of dust and decay, rather than flesh and blood, and Pip imagines that she is hanging by the neck from a wooden beam in the disused brewery building.**

The market-town, where Mr Pumblechook has his shop in the high street, and where Miss Havisham lives, is four miles from Pip's home. Pumblechook is "wretched company" for Pip on the morning he is to go to Miss Havisham's; he feeds him sparingly, and constantly tests his mental arithmetic, instead of attempting a meaningful conversation. He is pompous, greedy, self-satisfied and indolent; but justice is done, in a way, when Pip is admitted to Satis House and Estella tells Pumblechook that he is not wanted there.

Estella tells Pip that the name **Satis House** came from owners who felt they had all they wanted- "**they must have been easily satisfied in those days**". The struggle to survive- the struggle which Pip's dead brothers gave up as infants- seems to be a modern one. Certainly, most of the characters in the novel are dissatisfied with their lot; and **Pip learns that being wealthy is not a cure for the difficulties of life, whether this is the loneliness of the young, the bitterness of the old, or the isolation of the outsider**. While the original owners of Satis House may have been content with it, it does not meet Miss Havisham's expectations, and it is heavily barred to keep the outside world, the world of daylight and society, at bay.

Miss Havisham lives a fifteen-minute walk from Pumblechook's shop. Her house is "of old brick, and dismal", with "a great many iron bars". The downstairs windows are barred, and some upstairs have been walled up. The entrance to the courtyard at the front of the house is kept locked. The paving stones have grass growing between them (like gravestones in a churchyard?). The front door is never used- it, too, is chained up.

The interior is dark, and lit by candles. Just as there is no daylight or natural light, Pip observes that Miss Havisham "had withered like the dress, and like the flowers, and had no brightness left but the brightness of her sunken eyes". She has "shrunk to skin and bone". Pip had once seen "a skeleton in the ashes of a rich dress". Later, he narrates, he found out that "bodies buried in ancient times….fall to powder in the moment of being distinctly seen", and he thinks that if she had been exposed to daylight she would have turned to dust in the same way. She is wasted, a relic, barely alive in the emotional sense, and physically fragile.

Miss Havisham sits, "corpse-like", in her dressing-room, in an arm-chair, languidly, with "a watchful and brooding expression". Her clothing is made of rich satin, lace and silk, but it is faded, off-white. She has one shoe on; the other one is on the dressing-table and has never been worn. Her watch and the clock have stopped at twenty to nine, and items are strewn around exactly as they were on the day of her wedding; frozen in time, fossilised. It is the sense that time, or life, ended for Miss Havisham at that moment which makes her clothing look "so like grave-clothes" and "the long veil so like a shroud". Perceptively, Pip realises that she seems to have "dropped, body and soul, within and without, under the weight of a crushing blow".

When she speaks to Pip, she says that she has not seen the sun during his lifetime; and that her heart is "broken". She explains that she is tired and bored, and she has "a sick fancy" that she wants to see children playing. Pip is, as usual, polite; but he is intimidated by the strangeness and "melancholy" of the house. Miss Havisham says that the house is melancholy to her, too.

The cold wind reverberates around the house like the wind in the rigging of a ship- it is both shrill and howling. Miss Havisham's grief is just like this- cold, shrill and howling.

Estella lets Pip in; she has the keys, and is "very pretty and seemed very proud"; she and Pip are both about eight years old at this time, but Pip sees her as "beautiful and self-possessed", and as contemptuous as if she were a 21-year-old member of royalty. She addresses him repeatedly as "boy" (Pumblechook does, too); she is very inhospitable and rude; and, because she tells him so, Pip becomes acutely conscious, for the first time in his life, that he is a "common labouring-boy" with thick boots and coarse hands.

Her contemptuous attitude towards him is like a virus- "it became infectious, and I caught it". He is ashamed that he is not "genteelly brought up", and becomes tearful; Estella is gratified that her cruelty has made him feel so uncomfortable.

Miss Havisham holds jewels close to Estella to see how they look, and promises them to her "one day". Pip thinks he overhears her encouraging Estella to "break his heart"- as though Estella must avenge Miss Havisham's own emotional suffering on an innocent and helpless stranger, who is quite unconnected with her. She asks Pip what he thinks of Estella, whom he sums up as "very proud….very pretty….very insulting"; but he concedes that he might be willing to see her again. She tells him to come back in six days' time; she does not follow a calendar, or the days of the week.

Pip's emotional distress, when he gets out of the house, is because he is "sensitive", and because he has always known that his sister's violence and volatility is "unjust". Perhaps finding himself in a different setting, and seeing a different (though equally wrong) type of matriarchal behaviour, gives him a sense of perspective, so that he can see more objectively what is wrong with his own upbringing at the Gargerys'. Or perhaps he is in despair when he realises that, in the world beyond the village, he will still be treated harshly, regardless of how compliant he is with what people demand from him.

The last part of this chapter explores the area around Satis House more fully. The furniture of the former brewery is a "wilderness of empty casks", and there are empty stables, an empty pig-sty and an empty dovecote. There is an overgrown garden, full of weeds, but with signs that somebody walks there.

As he explores the deserted brewery, he catches sight of Estella there, walking on the beer barrels and climbing to the top of a light iron staircase. Here, Pip has his grotesque vision of Miss Havisham, with her one shoe on, hanging from a beam and calling to him. He refuses to let Estella see that he is afraid, as she lets him out through the locked gate. But she touches him, and asks why he is not crying; she knows what he is thinking and feeling. Her ability to control others- even at this young age- is the product of her intuition and her desire and training to be cruel. We see her, later, as a young adult, behaving in the same way, just as Pip's sensitivity stays with him, and just as Miss Havisham's grief at being left at the altar defines her behaviour from that moment onwards.

Pip walks home, reflecting on how inadequate he feels, merely because that is how Estella has judged him; he is suddenly ashamed of his circumstances, which he cannot control or alter, and which have never caused him distress before.

The empty casks in the brewery have "**a certain sour remembrance of better days** lingering about them". This is **a strikingly effective metaphor for Miss Havisham's determination to live in the past** and in the dark. It is **also a metaphor for Pip's feelings about his "old" life in the village**. Now that Estella has ridiculed and devalued it, to remember it is, in itself, a sour and bitter thing.

Chapter 9

Mrs Joe wants to know what Pip found at Miss Havisham's, and when his answers are too short, she shoves his face against the wall, the effect of which is that "Whitewash on the forehead hardens the brain into a state of obstinacy".

What we might call child abuse is a comical demonstration of how poor Mrs Joe is at verbal communication. Dickens struggles, though, to justify Pip's reticence, in the second paragraph. The argument that he might misrepresent Miss Havisham, as a justification for making up the tall tales he tells, is unconvincing. More satisfying is his teasing of Pumblechook, particularly as it becomes clear that he has never seen Miss Havisham himself, but has simply been allowed to speak to her from the corridor outside her room. Because he can confirm that the house is lit by candles, Pumblechook authenticates Pip's lies.

Pip describes her as "very tall and dark"; sitting in a black velvet coach; with four huge dogs, which eat out of a silver basket; playing with flags; and with a cupboard full of swords, pistols, jam and pills. Mrs Joe and Pumblechook are sure that Miss Havisham plans to benefit Pip in some way. They speculate on what form that might take; their expectations are running away with them.

Joe is predictably amazed by this picture of eccentricity; Pip regrets misleading him. **As we so often see with Dickens, the comical first half of the chapter gives way to a more serious scene**, in which Pip admits making up his description of Miss Havisham's. He explains to Joe his feelings of inferiority, prompted by Estella's merciless haughtiness, and says "the lies had come of it somehow, though I didn't know how". Joe disapproves, and points out that the way to escape being "common" is not to tell lies. **Being honest is the only way to "live well and die happy".** And Joe ruminates on whether it is better for people to stay within their own social class. He recognises that his wife is a social climber; while she is suspicious of education, she is not suspicious of gifts or money.

Pip looks back and sees this as a defining and "memorable" day for him- "it made great changes in me", and is the first link "of the long chain of iron or gold"- a metaphor for his life. *The reader is left to infer that it is not just Pip's new self-consciousness about his own poverty which is life-changing; it is meeting Estella, who becomes the obsession which preoccupies Pip for the rest of the novel.*

Summary - Chapters 6 – 9

These chapters begin with Pip realising **the power of the lie or of hiding the truth**; and they end with him constructing some unimportant but defiant untruths of his own. Estella's contempt for his coarse labouring-boy's hands and boots really hurts, but it is true that there is no proper schooling in the village and no prospect there of a better life.

Just as the unexpected arrival of Magwitch disturbed Pip's life deeply, Miss Havisham's summons does the same. She, too, is an apparition from a ghostly, alien world. Pip, in meeting each of them, loses control over his own life. His kindness to Magwitch is the basis of an extraordinary relationship, which ends with Magwitch's death. Pip's relationship with Miss Havisham follows the same path. Because neither of the adults makes their motive clear, Pip (and others) ignore the "evidence" and misunderstand the hidden truth.

Perhaps it is no accident that Pip suffers as a result of other people's non-disclosure only after he has treated Joe in the same way.

Dickens stresses that these chapters represent a fundamental change in Pip's life. That is quite hard to analyse, but the point is that, so long as Pip is not conscious of the disadvantages of his situation in life, he is content. As soon as Estella starts to mock his humble background, and as soon as Mrs Joe and Pumblechook start pushing him away from the village, Pip can no longer accept (as Joe does) that his place in life is settled.

He becomes unsettled, and his awareness of the drawbacks of his background drives him to a desire to improve himself. Moreover, Estella, the cold, self-assured beautiful child, is like a star he feels compelled to follow. The narrative demands that Pip's dissatisfaction (reinforced by Mrs Joe's ambition) is stronger than his fear of a world he is ill-equipped for.

Chapter 10

This is another chapter in two separate sections. The first tells us more about the so-called village "school" and Biddy's role in it. The second is a short, dramatic scene where Pip, Joe and Mr Wopsle meet the stranger (sent by Magwitch to repay Pip's generosity in Chapter 3) at the village pub, the Three Jolly Bargemen.

Pip now wants to escape his "common" background, so that he will be more acceptable to Estella. Biddy readily agrees to teach Pip everything she knows about writing and arithmetic.

When Pip calls at the pub to take Joe home, "the stranger turned his head and looked at me" as soon as Joe identifies Pip. In Chapter 3, the second convict (Compeyson) wore "a flat broad-brimmed low-crowned felt hat"; this man has "a flapping broad-brimmed traveller's hat". He rubs his leg and he stirs his drink with what Pip recognises as the file he had taken from Joe's forge and given to Magwitch. The "stranger" knows that the church is "right out on the marshes". He speaks differently from Magwitch (as Compeyson had, in the earlier scenes) and he does not have the odd click in his throat which identifies Magwitch. He is particularly keen to establish what the relationship is between Joe and Pip (son? nephew?).

He reveals to Pip his connection with Magwitch through the deliberate gesture of stirring his rum with Joe's file- "I knew that he knew my convict, the moment I saw the instrument"; because Joe and Mr Wopsle do not know about the file, they cannot make the same connection.

The "stranger" gives Pip what he says is a shilling wrapped in some crumpled paper; Mrs Joe assumes it is "a bad un" i.e. not genuine; but, of course, it is, and it is wrapped in two one pound notes. Joe runs back to the pub, thinking that the man gave them to Pip by mistake. He has left, so he cannot be found, and the money has to stay in safe keeping at Joe's until he comes back to the pub on some future occasion and they can be returned to him. He never returns to the pub, but he is on the coach, as a repeat offender, in Chapter 28, where he reveals that Magwitch has been given a life sentence for trying to escape from prison.

Pip has never seen the stranger before, but his non-verbal communication (like Magwitch's meaningful look, when he was recaptured) is enough to revive Pip's faded guilt over the pork pie episode. For Pip, the encounter is an unwelcome reminder "of the guiltily coarse and common thing it was, to be on secret terms……with convicts- a feature in my low career that I had previously forgotten", and it gives him nightmares.

For Pip, everything now must be related to his sense of social inferiority- this "low career". Receiving this money is concrete evidence of a secret bond between Pip and his convict; there is honour among criminals. It is a genteel or gentlemanly thing to repay your debts, but Pip will feel contaminated by the criminal source of the money (as he will do with Magwitch's fortune as a whole).

And, for the Gargerys, there is no question of taking or spending the money; they are poor but completely honest, and to be given such a large sum must be a mistake. In the adult world, people have a sense of morality and values. Pip is a child, and **he now feels hopelessly uncomfortable, caught between the two worlds of being "coarse and common", and aspiring to be worthy of Estella's elevated society**. He is wrong to see the world he has come from as inferior or lacking in honour. He is also wrong, it turns out, to think of Estella as a creature from a better world.

It is his sense of discomfort and shame which had led him to lie about what he found at Miss Havisham's; in a sense, what is there is a fantasy or a dream, which Pumblechook and the others cannot share because they have no access to it, and too little imagination. When he has an unaccustomed element of power (information) over the adults who have habitually patronized him, Pip uses it dishonestly. We neither judge him for this, nor disapprove, because he is a child, and because they deserve it, and it is relatively harmless. But we now think of Pip as a child who has aspirations which may lead him into difficulties, as he tries to escape from what has been, until now, his comfort zone.

Chapter 11

Pip returns to Satis House, as instructed, six days later. Estella adopts the same superior manner with him as before. He has to wait in an ante-room with four strangers, to whom he is not introduced; they do not talk to him, but it is clear to Pip that they are "all toadies and humbugs". Comically, Pip as narrator says that none of them will admit that any of the others is a toady, because, if they did, that would make them one too!

The descriptions are unflattering; Camilla is like Mrs Joe, but "older, and……of a blunter cast of features…..the dead wall of her face….was very blank and high". She is bored, or tired, because she twice suppresses a yawn. Her catch-phrase is "The idea!". She continually complains that she is ruining her health by waking up during the night worrying about her extended family. Her husband (Raymond) remarks- ironically- that she worries so much that one of her legs is becoming shorter than the other. Camilla's expressions of self-dramatising emotion are treated mercilessly here by Dickens; and Mrs Joe, in Chapter 15, works herself into the same state of outrage, with disastrous results.

The description of Sarah Pocket is delayed until the middle of the chapter- "a little dry brown corrugated old woman, with a small face that might have been made of walnut shells, and a large mouth like a cat's". Pip, as narrator, adjudges her "blandly vicious" and observes her "artful slipperiness".

On a visit at Miss Havisham's, Estella stops abruptly, confronts Pip, and demands to know, "in a taunting manner", whether she is pretty. He says she is, but that she is not as "insulting" as before- for which she slaps him (in Chapter 8, Pip had described Estella to Miss Havisham as pretty, and insulting, and proud) . It is worth remembering that both Pip and Estella are still very young – they would be primary school age children today- and their taunts (in a playground of today, say) might be frequent and without much meaning.

Even so, this is the first of a number of incidents of unprovoked violence in the novel. Estella calls him "you little coarse monster" and "you little wretch". Pip judges, as narrator, that "I was inwardly crying for her then, and I know what I know of the pain she cost me afterwards". **In one sense, the novel is about ways in which emotional pain hinders productivity (Pip, Miss Havisham, Estella)**; the characters who seem to have less complex emotional lives are the ones whose lives are economically more successful (Magwitch, Jaggers, Pumblechook, Wemmick). Estella bullies Pip verbally, much as Mrs Joe has, physically; and she accuses him of "telling upstairs"- of telling tales to Miss Havisham. Pip is perversely loyal to Estella, and perversely disloyal to Joe, later. When Magwitch becomes dependent on him, he is truly loyal- and for the right reasons.

Pip meets the lawyer Jaggers on the stairs at Miss Havisham's house. Jaggers is "burly…dark…large…his eyes were set very deep in his head, and were disagreeably sharp and suspicious". He has the mannerisms of biting "the side of his great forefinger". He smells of scented soap.

Miss Havisham has so many visitors because it is her birthday, although she will not have it referred to in conversation. Pip prefers to work rather than to play; she directs him to wait in the room opposite, which is dominated by a long table with a centre-piece "heavily overhung with cobwebs", under which her wedding cake still lies. The room is inhabited by spiders and beetles; he can hear mice behind the skirting-boards. Pip's "work" is to walk her round and round the room- another expression of **her obsessive/compulsive behaviour and her self-imposed entrapment in her private world of resentment.**

She has a "withered hand"; with her "crutch-headed stick…..she looked like the Witch of the place". She announces, in a macabre way, that when she is dead she will be laid out on the table; "they shall come and look at me here". Dickens subverts the dramatic seriousness of this, by having young Pip think that "she might get upon the table then and there and die at once". Her hand twitches. She speaks in imperatives. She is much less sympathetic here than before. She speaks to her hangers-on "with exceeding sharpness". She strikes the table with her stick to indicate where they are each to stand "when you come to feast upon me"; and she reproves them for the constant complaints they make about the absent Matthew (Pocket).

Although we do not know what the family relationship is, we understand that the visitors are here, not to celebrate, but to ingratiate themselves, from self-interest, as they want to inherit Miss Havisham's estate (making fun of the greed of heir-hunters is an old comic tradition in literature; it is, for instance, the theme of Ben Jonson's celebrated play "Volpone", which was first staged at the start of the 17th century,).

Estella brings in the other visitors while Pip's tour of the room continues. Camilla takes pleasure in Miss Havisham's put-down to Sarah Pocket, but she is treated equally viciously herself.

Miss Havisham has no axe to grind with Pip, and explains to him that her birthday commemorates the day on which the wedding paraphernalia were brought to where they still are, untouched and unmoved. In a rare moment of self-disclosure, she says that mice have gnawed at the wedding cake, "and sharper teeth than teeth of mice have gnawed at me". This extends the **animalistic and cannibalistic tone**. She feels that she is being eaten alive by emotional betrayal, and that she will be feasted on by her relatives when she is dead. If she dies on her birthday, that will complete the "curse" on "him"- the man who broke his promise to marry her. Much later, in chapter 42, we learn that the man who exploited, cheated and betrayed her is Compeyson; for now however, it is not relevant who he was, as our attention is on the effect the (non) event continues to have on Miss Havisham.

After a long, "heavy" silence, dominated by the reverberations of Miss Havisham's bitterness, she recovers her self-control "in an instant", and reverts to the familiar charade of Estella beating Pip at cards, while Miss Havisham looks for evidence that Estella's beauty can be enhanced by jewellery, to exert power over men or boys.

Once Miss Havisham has set the date of Pip's next visit, he is let out, and explores the garden; when he looks in at a window, he finds himself "exchanging a broad stare with a pale young gentleman with red eyelids and light hair". The boy comes out, has a spotty face, and is "inky" from his studies indoors; he immediately challenges Pip to fight him, "in a manner at once light-hearted, businesslike, and bloodthirsty".

Pip feels inferior, in height and technique, but the fight is completely one-sided; the other boy has a nosebleed, then a black eye, but refuses to give in. The fight is a comical mismatch- "I am sorry to record that the more I hit him, the harder I hit him"- and it only ends when Pip's opponent bangs his head on the wall.

Pip is struck by the sense that the boy is "brave and innocent" and that he himself is "a species of savage young wolf, or other wild beast". They part civilly, without finding out who they each are. The fight, whilst shocking to us today, is presented as just something that boys (then) would do, and purely for sport. Just as both Magwitch's and Molly's identities are delayed, so is this boy's (Herbert). And just as Magwitch is first defined by his fearsome uncouthness, and (later when we meet her) Molly will be characterised by her physical strength, Herbert's brave optimism and resilience is a good indication of his whole personality, as we come to know him.

Estella has watched the fight, and has been delighted and excited by the violence (a foreshadowing of her awful marriage to Drummle later in the novel). She invites Pip to kiss her on her cheek, but it seems patronising to him, because he is again so acutely conscious of his social inferiority- "I felt that the kiss was given to the coarse common boy as a piece of money might have been".

The end of this chapter brings a break in the serialisation of the novel, which was its original method of publication. The same had applied at the end of Chapter 2, Chapter 4, Chapter 5, Chapter 7, Chapter 8 and Chapter 10. The division into sections is quite even; in a modern edition each of these separate episodes is about 12 pages long. It may be helpful to think of each of these instalments as being **like a half-hour episode of a long-running soap opera on television**; each episode will have some of the same characters, and there has to be a dramatic cliff-hanger at the end of every instalment, to make the reader or viewer want to pick the story up again.

Kissing Estella is a cliff-hanging, dramatic moment. So is running to the marshes with food for Magwitch (Chapter 2); the arrival of the soldiers just when Mrs Joe is about to find out that the pork pie has disappeared (Chapter 4); the recapture of Magwitch (Chapter 5); Pip's departure to meet Miss Havisham for the first time (Chapter 7); and his awareness, for the first time, of his humble status as "a common labouring-boy" (Chapter 8).

But this alone is not enough to shape a long novel which must sustain our interest over more than 450 pages. What we have seen Dickens do, in this first quarter of the novel, is to set up **a number of puzzles, or mysterious threads**. What does Miss Havisham want from Pip? How will Pip's relationship with Estella develop? Will Pip succeed in breaking away from the poverty and lack of education which he feels so holds him back? And if so, how?

The novel before Dickens had often been concerned with **the growth of its hero or heroine, to maturity, or independence, or marriage**- overcoming problems and obstacles along the way. In one sense, this is what Dickens is doing with Pip; he is maturing as his social world enlarges.

But Dickens does more than this. The early part of the story is full of characters whose names we do not even know yet (Magwitch. Compeyson. Jaggers. Herbert Pocket), and characters whose significance to the plot is not yet clear. This means that, as readers, we feel some of the same **puzzlement** Pip feels, as the rather brutal life of his early childhood broadens into a world physically and emotionally away from home.

Narrating the novel from the point of view of Pip is a master stroke. Pip is both young at the time of the action so far, and also quite knowing, because he is relating the events from the perspective of adulthood, looking back. This allows Dickens to highlight the humour in some episodes, as well as Pip's feeling of vulnerability, and the unpleasantness and/or hypocrisy of characters like Mrs Joe, Pumblechook, Miss Havisham, Estella, Sarah Pocket and Camilla.

There is a striking kernel of goodness around Joe, whom Pip freely concedes he idolises. Joe is a good and decent man who is under fire from his wife and handicapped by his lack of sophistication. But he is not resentful, or judgmental, or selfish; and no matter how provocative Mrs Joe is, he will not betray the morality he developed during his own childhood. Joe is at peace with himself and the world he lives in. His acceptance of his lot is stronger than his ambition to improve it; he feels he has nothing to prove to anyone. The meaning of the novel is beginning to assert itself; when we go back to the second paragraph of Chapter 1, and Pip's five dead brothers "who gave up trying to get a living, exceedingly early in that universal struggle", we realise that **financial security is a false goal. Emotional happiness is much more elusive, and more worthwhile.**

Chapter 12

Pip's conscience and imagination had been haunted by what might happen as a consequence of his "stealing" the pork pie for Magwitch. Now, he is haunted by a sense that, in winning the fight against the boy who had challenged him to it, he has broken the law, because "village boys.....ravaging the houses of gentlefolks….lay themselves open to severe punishment". His sense of social inferiority conditions him to expect the worst.

Dickens uses the phrase "the pale young gentleman" five times in the first paragraph, and then twice more, for comic effect. He uses three successive rhetorical questions in the second paragraph to do justice to the force of Pip's fears, while at the same time making the reader appreciate that they are exaggerated; Pip is brave yet timid.

When Pip returns to Miss Havisham's, by arrangement, there is no sign of the pale boy.

For the next "eight to ten months", Pip pushes her around the two rooms in a wheeled chair for up to three hours at a time. Miss Havisham takes no interest in Pip's aspiration to educate himself- "she seemed to prefer my being ignorant".

Estella's behaviour remains as puzzling as ever to Pip. Miss Havisham seems to "enjoy it greedily" when Pip confirms that Estella is becoming "prettier and prettier"; she treats Estella with "lavish fondness", and Pip thinks he hears her whispering an ominous invocation in her ear-

"Break their hearts my pride and hope, break their hearts and have no mercy!" –

just as Pip had thought he heard her telling Estella, in Chapter 8, "you can break his heart".

If Miss Havisham's motivation- turning Estella into a man-hater, to compensate for her own rejection at the altar- is clear to us, it is not yet clear to Pip. It is not an accident that she embodies this meanness, lack of nobility, and, above all, negative emotional energy.

The **characters who are poor- Joe and Biddy, Herbert and the early Magwitch- are all generous emotionally**. **Those with money- Miss Havisham, Estella, Jaggers and Pumblechook- are ungenerous** in terms of the goodwill they offer to other people.

Miss Havisham's creeping influence on Pip's thinking extends to adopting Joe's working song "Old Clem". Pip feels inhibited from talking to Joe about Satis House; but he tells Biddy "everything"; why this was the case, Pip tells us "I did not know then, though I think I know now".

The reason is that Biddy has great good sense and natural wisdom beyond her years, despite the fact that all her possessions fit into "a small speckled box" (Chapter 16). With the wisdom of adulthood, Pip knows that he should have married Biddy, who would have been his true soul mate- although, if he had, we would not have the novel!

Pumblechook and Mrs Joe continually indulge in "nonsensical speculations" on Pip's "prospects", that is, whether Miss Havisham will be his patron in some way, and what that might lead to. Pumblechook's original idea- that Miss Havisham might sponsor Pip's apprenticeship- eventually proves correct.

Pumblechook starts to attract a number of **damning adjectives**, here, and in the next few chapters- "the miserable man", "a spectacle of imbecility", a "fearful Impostor", "that abject hypocrite", "that basest of swindlers", "the villain", "swindling", "that detested seedsman" , "that diabolical corn-chandler" and "that swindling Pumblechook, exalted into the beneficent contriver of the whole occasion" – **because he pretends** to be the architect of the twenty-five guineas which Miss Havisham provides to set up Pip's apprenticeship to Joe in Chapter 13. All he has done is to suggest Pip, when Miss Havisham asked "if he knew of a boy to go and play there".

When Miss Havisham issues the summons for Joe to see her, with Pip, Mrs Joe "went on the Rampage", which means that she cleans the house "to a terrible extent". She uses cleaning and temperamental outbursts as an inarticulate substitute for expressing her feelings- here, the fear of change, coupled with excitement about what may lie ahead for Pip. Perhaps she is disappointed, too, that Miss Havisham does not choose to help Pip with "property", so that "this boy's fortune may be made by his going", as she had put it in Chapter 7.

Chapter 13

Miss Havisham has decided that, as Pip is growing taller (and therefore ready to have a job), he should be apprenticed to Joe formally; she **has no intention of gentrifying Pip**.

Dickens exploits the comic potential of the meeting of Miss Havisham and Joe to the full; Joe is dressed in his uncomfortable best clothes, and "like some extraordinary bird", "standing…..speechless". He cannot speak directly to Miss Havisham, who asks him a series of questions. He answers, instead, as if Pip were asking them. Because of his embarrassment (social inferiority again) Joe's manner of speaking is unnatural, combining "forcible argumentation, strict confidence, and great politeness" – again, the repetition of this phrase highlights the comedy. But Pip is embarrassed, because Estella's "eyes laughed mischievously" at Joe's fumbling for words.

Miss Havisham establishes that Joe had not intended to make taking Pip as his apprentice conditional on being paid to do so; she looks at Joe, and, just as Magwitch had looked at Pip, and the stranger in the pub had looked at Pip, this look is penetrating – she "glanced at him as if she understood what he really was, better than I had thought possible, seeing what he was there".

What she sees is Joe's generosity, honesty and integrity. Therefore she gives him the twenty-five guineas, which she has set aside beforehand. Joe is "absolutely out of his mind with the wonder awakened in him by her strange figure and the strange room". He thanks her, through Pip, and stresses that the money is "welcome, though never looked for", and he bursts into expressing the almost prayer-like hope that he and Pip will "do our duty, both on us by one and another, and by them which your liberal present- have- conweyed", before running out of words to say what he feels.

Miss Havisham calls Joe back, to make it clear that she will give Pip no more money, that what she has paid him is what Pip has earned for his services to her, and that Joe is responsible for him now. Joe walks up the stairs instead of down; his disorientation is amusing, and he has found the meeting "astonishing".

With typical regard for his wife, Joe pretends that Miss Havisham sends Mrs Joe her compliments, and an apology for not being well enough to meet her; and that she wants the money handed over to Mrs Joe. All of this is, of course, an invention, to make Mrs Joe feel more important and respected than she really is.

Joe reveals the actual sum of money in three suspenseful stages (it's not ten pounds, it's not twenty pounds, it's twenty-five). Pumblechook claims to have arranged this, by impressing on Miss Havisham that that was the right amount of money to give- only Pip and the reader know that Pumblechook has never met Miss Havisham, because he could not contradict Pip's made up description of her in Chapter 9 as "very tall and dark". Pumblechook does not know what she looks like because, when he goes to Satis House to pay his rent, he is never admitted to her room.

Pumblechook has always been oppressive towards Pip, and he insists that they go to the magistrates' court immediately, so that Pip's apprenticeship is made legally binding, which means that Pip will be "liable to imprisonment if I played at cards, drank strong liquors, kept late hours or bad company, or indulged in other vagaries".

Pumblechook's dishonesty, in taking the credit for Miss Havisham's gift, and Mrs Joe's greed ("grasping the money") are a discordant note; they detract from the optimism and goodness which Joe had brought to the occasion. When Pip finally escapes the adults, and goes to bed, he feels "truly wretched" because he knows that his heart is not in becoming a blacksmith.

The celebratory meal at the Blue Boar, which Pip's sister insists on, has the same cast as the Christmas meal in Chapter 4. Again, the way the adults behave to Pip shows how little they care about him. We feel, almost as acutely as Pip himself, that he has grown out of what little they offer- a safe home, and limitless examples of patronising, harsh and unsympathetic behaviour to the only child amongst them.

Summary - Chapters 10-13

At the end of Chapter 9, Pip had developed a drive to escape from the village and from his social ineptness; he aspires to the higher "level" of sophistication which he attributes to Estella and Miss Havisham. This is ironic, with hindsight, as Estella is Magwitch's daughter and Miss Havisham had been on the point of marrying Compeyson**; their ties to the lowest of society, the criminal, are much more authentic than Pip's, which are only accidental.**

Pip hopes to improve himself by asking Biddy to educate him. This will be a slow and limited process. He hopes that Miss Havisham will sponsor an education for him- "I enlarged upon my knowing nothing and wanting to know everything, in the hope that she might offer some help towards that desirable end". His education and improvement is a desirable end for Pip because he sees it as putting him on the same "level" as Estella; but that is of no interest to Miss Havisham, who simply sees Pip as a guinea pig or laboratory rat on whom Estella is to practice the scientific, heart-breaking powers which she is developing.

Despite Estella's high-handedness, and the dysfunctional nature of Miss Havisham, Pip dreads the blacksmith's apprenticeship he is sold into, because his aspirations go beyond a life at the forge, doing what the uneducated and limited Joe, and his uneducated, limited and alcoholic father, have done. He wants to be socially mobile, but he is being pushed back into the position he has come from. This question of the value of education in promoting social mobility through the acquisition of professional skills (and expanding the further education sector) is still very relevant to us today.

Joe persists in a simple way of looking at the world. He clings to the fact that working with him at the forge ("what larks" they would have!) "were the great wish of your (Pip's) heart". Joe has spent his whole life on the marshes and he has no curiosity about the possible existence of a better one beyond the village.

Chapter 14

Pip expands on the sense that **his childhood, and the contentment that came with it, is at an end**, as his apprenticeship to Joe begins. He sees the limitations of his surroundings clearly, and he is sensitive, above all, to the sense of shame he would feel if Estella should "find him out", look in at the window of the forge when he is "at my grimiest and commonest", and "exult over me and despise me". He both fears and hopes that she will "come at last", and he imagines he can see her "face in the fire, with her pretty hair fluttering in the wind and her eyes scorning me".

Estella is, of course, not intended for Pip, and not interested in him.

Pip knows that to feel "ashamed" of his home is "ungracious", but the feeling "miserable" is real. So is his sister's temper. Pip's childish belief "in the forge as the glowing road to manhood and independence" no longer stands up. As he concedes, whether the shattering of that sense of security and belonging was because of Miss Havisham, his sister, or himself, is irrelevant. Once we have grown out of that uncritical fondness for our childhood surroundings, and seen their drawbacks, there is no going back to them.

Knowing that he was "bound" to the forge was like a crushingly heavy weight, or "a thick curtain" which shuts out "interest and romance". It was Joe's work ethic which kept Pip from running away to join the army or the navy. Joe is, as always, "amiable, honest-hearted, duty-doing…plain contented"; Pip is "restlessly aspiring…. discontented", but cannot articulate what it is he wants. All he knows is that he does not want Estella to despise him.

Chapter 15

Pip's imagination continues to be preoccupied with Estella, Miss Havisham, "the strange house and the strange life", and he suggests to Joe that he should visit Miss Havisham to express his gratitude to her. With a comical slip of the tongue, he calls her "Miss Est-Havisham", and so betrays his real focus- seeing Estella. Joe thinks that a visit my be presumptuous, because Miss Havisham had been so insistent that there was to be no coming back for more money, and that Pip's time at Satis House was at an end (now that Estella had tried her weapons out on him successfully, there was nothing more to be learned from that experiment).

We can understand why Pip's thoughts are distracted from his home surroundings; he is **frustrated by his lack of access to education, and those he lives amongst, including Biddy, have nothing more to teach him**. The little Pip has managed to learn, he has tried to share with Joe, not to help him, but to make him "less ignorant and common"- in case Estella were to see him again.

As usual, Joe supports Pip in what he wants to do (despite his own doubts about the wisdom of the intended visit); he is aware of the social niceties and etiquette- the need not to step beyond the bounds of class- in a way Pip is not.

Now we encounter Orlick for the first time. He is a "journeyman" or labourer whom Joe employs; he is aged about 25, strong, morose and "always slouching", and he lodges out on the marshes. His living there, and the way he likes to frighten Pip (by saying the devil requires a boy to be sacrificed on the forge fire every seven years), ally him in our mind with the criminal temperament of (the still unnamed) Magwitch.

But, where Magwitch frightened Pip simply to save himself from even more acute physical pain and hunger, Orlick has always disliked Pip, and may perhaps now think that Pip's apprenticeship to Joe threatens his own job. This resentment prefigures Orlick's attempt to kill Pip in Chapter 53.

Orlick insists that, if Pip is to have half a day off work to go to see Miss Havisham, he should, too, so that he, too, can "go up-town". Joe, being the benevolent man he is, allows this, much to the displeasure of Mrs Joe, who has been "standing silent in the yard, within hearing". She is "beginning to work herself into a mighty rage" because she does not agree with paid holidays. Orlick trades insults with her, and she orchestrates her own increasingly hysterical response. She insists that Joe, who is "standing by", must "defend" her, by fighting Orlick. There is a conscious reference to, and echo of, Pip's fight with the boy (who turns out to be Herbert Pocket) in the garden of Satis House. Mrs Joe watches the fight, then faints (Estella watches Pip's fight, then allows him to kiss her on the cheek, because she is excited). Orlick, like "the pale young gentleman", has a damaged and bloody nose (see Chapter 12); and there appears to be no animosity from the loser to the winner. But **Orlick's brooding,**

thuggish sense of inferiority is a world away from Herbert's gentlemanly absence of resentment.

Here, the narrative changes abruptly; Pip is at his destination, Satis House; Miss Havisham receives him coolly at first, and tells him that Estella is not there, because she is being "educated to be a lady", and is "far out of reach". She asks Pip whether he feels that he has "lost her", and does so with "malignant enjoyment", a "disagreeable laugh", and a dismissal. The effect of this is to leave Pip feeling even more dissatisfied with his situation than he was before.

With another equally abrupt change from one short scene to another, Pip bumps into Mr Wopsle, who takes him with him to see Pumblechook for a self-dramatised reading of George Lillo's tragedy of George Barnwell, a melodrama about a murderous apprentice. Wopsle (the actor) and Pumblechook (the self-styled moral guardian of Pip) behave in a way which is true to their shallow, obsessive and one-dimensional characters. Just as the fact that the Christmas meal had featured pork had enabled the two men to compare Pip with "swine" and "squeakers", here, the simple and accidental fact that Pip is an apprentice allows them to treat him as guilty of murder by association, because the melodrama is about an apprentice. Pumblechook will still be repeating the lecture he gave, that first Christmas, on greed, ingratitude and prodigality, in Chapter 58, when Pip is completely grown up.

More importantly, this episode generates the passage of time (until 11pm) which enables Orlick to attack Mrs Joe, and effect an alibi of sorts by joining them on the walk back and claiming he had gone into the town too. Pip does not know (at first) who has been attacked, or who the attacker might be; the assumption everyone makes is that it is **convicts** who have escaped earlier in the day. With a taut economy of style, Dickens lets us see- only in the last sentence of the chapter-that Mrs Joe is lying unconscious on the kitchen floor, having been hit on the head from behind "by a tremendous blow".

It is an interesting question how many of us, on a first reading of the novel, identify Orlick as Mrs Joe's assailant. He seems thuggish and inarticulate, disrespectful towards Joe, moodily insolent and potentially aggressive; and he has been involved in a war of words with Mrs Joe, which ended with Joe humiliating him in the fistfight. That fight was inevitable, given her histrionics and Joe's principled morality about the respect and protection women are entitled to. On the other hand, he is an employee, trusted and treated well by Joe.

Perhaps the fairest judgment is that we tend, thus far, to believe that the working people in this novel have an innate nobility; they respect the property of others, and they do not use violence to take what they do not have- as we saw when Mrs Joe tried to return the two pound notes to the stranger. We do not credit Orlick with a rounded enough personality to suppose he could feel humiliated or insecure to the extent of hurting a defenceless woman. Nor do we think that he is malignant enough to carry out such a vicious and unprovoked attack.

The fact that convicts are on the loose again makes it easy to assume they must be responsible, as they could have broken into the Gargerys'. But our feelings about this are ambivalent, because **we have already seen, in Magwitch, a convict who is not stereotypically wicked.**

One of the striking characteristics of Dickens' style in these opening chapters is **the mixture of the realistic and the caricature or cartoonish**. Some characters are one-dimensional, others three-dimensional. And, **in the narrative tone, we find a mixture of major and minor keys; of optimism and unease; of hope and anxiety; of sudden drama, and reflection.** This is only possible because Pip narrates his childhood experiences from the perspective of adulthood, though that makes his recall of such minute detail, especially in the dialogue, a leap of faith for us! However, this is a novel … so this allowance is made, because it gives us such an enjoyable read.

Chapter 16

We are used by now to Dickens' use of **unexpected twists** and apparently unmotivated behaviour to **add to the sense of mystery**, and so to motivate us to read on. Here, Biddy helps to identify Orlick as Mrs Joe's attacker; but Mrs Joe does not accuse him, or confront him (perhaps because she did not see him, as she was hit from behind), but seeks to conciliate him.

It is ironic if she is trying to apologise to him for her histrionics, which led to Joe beating him up, without knowing that he had avenged himself by attacking her. The alternative is that, like Molly towards Jaggers, she is cowed into submission from fear-having lost the power of speech, she cannot "denounce him", but she is in a wordless terror that he may lose his temper again, and attack her again, or the others.

The subtext here is a little like the satirical treatment of the travesty which passes for the village's informal education via "that preposterous female" Mr Wopsle's great-aunt; this time, it is the police who are treated as figures of fun, for their incompetence and their suspicion of Joe, whose intelligence they overestimate ("they had to a man concurred in regarding him as one of the deepest spirits they had ever encountered"). **When law enforcement cannot distinguish between the fundamentally good (Joe) and the fundamentally bad (Orlick) there is little likelihood that justice will be done.**

In the first half of this chapter, we learn more about the crime- it took place between 10 and 11pm. Magwitch's old leg-iron has been put at the scene to imply that the escaped convicts are responsible; but one of them has been recaptured before the time of the attack, still wearing his leg-irons; the leg-iron has not been removed recently; and nothing has been taken from the house. Pip wonders whether the attacker is the stranger who gave him the two pound notes, and stirred his drink with Joe's file, but he would have had no need to attack Mrs Joe in order to have his money back. This leaves Orlick as the prime suspect, but Pip dismisses the possibility because his sister "had quarrelled with him, and with everybody else about her, ten thousand times".

Pip rationalises his reluctance to tell Joe about the Magwitch connection- which would rule out a convict as the attacker- on the grounds that "**the secret….had….grown into me and become a part of myself**", and that Joe might not believe him, or would think less of him if he did. Internalising your feelings about past events in your life which cause you guilt or grief, as Pip does here, is a behaviour he shares with Joe (whose acquiescence in his wife's volatile and overwrought behaviour indirectly leads to her disability and death) and with Miss Havisham, who has never resolved her bitterness over being abandoned at the altar, and who therefore has a concept of marriage which is equally misguided as Joe's.

The second half of the chapter presents us with the concrete effects of the attack on Mrs Joe. Her vision and hearing are impaired; her memory is damaged, and very poor, and she cannot speak. In spite of these very real and devastating consequences, we do not really sympathise with Mrs Joe, because she has been so antagonistic herself.

Rather than dwell on the sadness of her suffering, Dickens makes her difficulty in communicating effectively a source of humour ("mutton instead of medicine…the baker for bacon…tar to toast and tub") rather than frustration or tragedy.

The death of Mr Wopsle's great-aunt, who, euphemistically, "conveniently ……conquered a confirmed habit of living", brings Biddy to live with Joe and Pip ("with a small speckled box containing the whole of her worldly effects"). Biddy at first relieves Joe's distress by enabling him to get out to the pub; in the long term, she becomes the compassionate and reasonable wife he had always deserved. Biddy's unaffected poverty, goodness and constructive attitude is the polar opposite of the snobbish, exploitative meanness of spirit which Miss Havisham cultivates in Estella, and of the self-imposed martyrdom Mrs Joe indulged in.

Just as Mrs Joe's "rampaging" domestic violence ends when someone is violent towards her, so Estella's emotional abuse of young men is requited by the emotional and physical abuse Bentley Drummle inflicts on her towards the end of the novel.

It is interesting that (leaving out Miss Skiffins, who is not a fully developed character), among a set of otherwise damaged and damaging female characters, Biddy is the only one who is completely balanced and sane.

The chapter ends with **another mystery**; Biddy solves the puzzle of the meaning of the letter "T" (representing a hammer, and thus the forge) which Mrs Joe draws on the slate, and is "exultant" when she realises that it signifies that the attacker is Orlick. Orlick returns to the house, and we expect him to be confronted by the uncomfortable truth of his crime, just as Pip almost was, on Christmas Day, when he had taken the pork pie for Magwitch. But Mrs Joe behaves to Orlick like "a child towards a hard master"- she is submissive and eager to please him, and does not take the opportunity to "denounce him". We tend to presume that her memory is so damaged that she cannot make the right connection between Orlick and his crime. Mrs Joe had been unable to express her feelings in words to Joe and Pip, and had used violent cleaning and physical violence instead. **Perhaps this is Dickens having fun with us, the reader, and so Mrs Joe loses the power of speech because she had never used it properly when she had it**.

Chapter 17

This is an important chapter. It adds depth to Pip's thoughts- and it confirms that his ambition to become a "gentleman", and thus be acceptable in the illusory world of Estella and Miss Havisham, is a motivation which has such force that he cannot accept the positive aspects of his life at the forge or settle for what it offers. This now includes a relationship with Biddy- who, amusingly, but truthfully, tells Pip that she would settle for him, because she is "not over-particular".

Biddy, for all her lack of opportunity, which Dickens encapsulates as "that miserable old bundle….always to be dragged and shouldered", is like Joe; she does not seek to deter Pip, even when her instinctive wisdom tells her that his intentions will be frustrated and his choices are wrong. She **has no desire to persuade him to adjust his own expectations; he must do so, by making his own mistakes.**

Pip experiences a continual inner conflict. He feels "vexation and distress" because he is "disgusted with my calling and my life". He is "dissatisfied and uncomfortable" because Estella has made him aware that he is "coarse and common".

Biddy is invariably right about people. She discerns that Orlick admires her (ludicrously- as ludicrously as Pip admires Estella, "dreadfully"); she discerns that Estella is "not worth gaining over".

Pip has begun to appreciate Biddy's qualities ("pleasant and wholesome and sweet-tempered…curiously thoughtful and attentive eyes; eyes that were very pretty and very good…..the wisest of girls….never insulting, or capricious") **but his judgment is shallow**, because he is dazzled by Estella- "she was not beautiful- she was common, and could not be like Estella".

Pip feels that Biddy is "extraordinary" because she has escaped from her former "hopeless circumstances……in the miserable little shop", and so he confesses his "lunatic" social ambition to her- he **wants to become a gentleman, in order to be worthy of Estella**. She goes straight to the heart of the issue, asking him "don't you think you are happier as you are?"

As the narrator, Pip excuses his faulty thinking by describing himself as "a poor dazed village lad". Although he knows Biddy is right, he cannot accept it, because he has been bewitched by Estella; the potential attraction of living "naturally and wholesomely" has none of the dark attraction of "being despised by Estella".

Pip so disregards Biddy that he talks openly about the desirability of getting himself to fall in love with her, as a solution to his feeling "miserable"; Biddy predicts, accurately, that he "never will". She is pragmatic and clear-sighted and wise where he is fanciful and unrealistic and mistaken. Pip's rational side knows that "Biddy was immeasurably better than Estella", but his emotional side is liable to being devastated by "some confounding remembrance of the Havisham days.….like a destructive missile". He even harbours an irrational thought that "perhaps after all Miss Havisham was going to make my fortune"- despite all the unambiguous and unmistakable evidence to the contrary.

The child Pip takes a stronger dislike to Orlick, because of his liking for Biddy and her dislike of him. The adult Pip tells us that if Orlick had not been a fixture at home, because of Mrs Joe's insistence on seeing him and being pleasant to him, he would have tried to get Joe to dismiss him; and, with a hint to future parts of the plot, Dickens reveals- with characteristic irony- that "He quite understood and reciprocated my good intentions, as I had reason to know thereafter". Orlick hatches his own plan, to get rid of Pip for good (the instinct is the same as Compeyson's, to get rid of Magwitch- a mixture of fear, resentment and self-preservation).

The feelings Dickens gives Pip here have an inwardness and authenticity which must surely reflect **Dickens' own emotional conflict**- he abandoned his wife for the young actress Ellen Ternan. Through Pip's not altogether convincing attraction to Estella, Dickens is articulating his own struggle with the power of the unsuitable to attract, and to distort the value of what deserves to be appreciated (for Biddy, read Dickens' wife Kate).

Pip's whole process of growing up is about learning, through experience, to distinguish between the meretricious and what has lasting value. It is also about **overcoming the familiarity or even comfort of being controlled by others** – usually parent/surrogate parent figures (Mrs Joe, Miss Havisham, Pumblechook, Magwitch)-so that you can determine your own identity and fate in life. If Estella were capable of being "gained over" by Pip merely by his acquiring the manner of a gentleman, he, like Joe, would be importing the wrongs and damage of his own growing up into his adult relationship, and making it dysfunctional; he would be allowing Estella the degree of control over him that Miss Havisham had allowed Compeyson over her.

Pip's romantic obsession actually makes it impossible both for him to win Estella and for him to enjoy the secure and equal relationship with the wise and stable Biddy which would be best for him. **No-one feels the need to fight over Biddy; wherever Estella goes, there is fighting and conflict** (Pip/Herbert, Pip/Drummle, Estella/Drummle). But **Pip- like Joe**, until he marries Biddy- **embraces the volatile, the abusive, the exciting, the unreasonable, the demeaning (Mrs Joe/ Estella), because that is the model he has grown up with, and which he sees as the natural state of things.**

Chapter 18

Three years later, when Pip has just turned 18, Joe and Pip are in the pub, listening to Mr Wopsle dramatizing an account of a murder trial in the newspaper, in his declamatory, Shakespearian style.

"A strange gentleman" is looking on, "coldly and sarcastically" and with "an expression of contempt on his face". We know, at least as soon as Pip does, that this is Jaggers, the lawyer, because "he bit the side of a great forefinger ", just as he had done on Miss Havisham's stairs in Chapter 11. But we do not know his name or occupation until he identifies himself privately to Joe and Pip later in this chapter.

He exposes Wopsle as a woolly thinker and a negligent juror. He impresses on the audience in the pub the fact that **justice and the legal system are not a theatrical entertainment but a matter of the utmost seriousness, because there is a risk that the innocent are found guilty**, and he cross-examines Wopsle "with an air of authority not to be disputed".

Pip now recognises Jaggers as the stranger he had met at Miss Havisham's, not just from his appearance and features, but from "the smell of scented soap" on his hands. **Because of the (purely coincidental) location of their meeting, Pip assumes that**

"Miss Havisham was going to make my fortune on a grand scale", despite all of the emphasis she has put on the fact that, Pip's birthdays apart, their connection is over (even more so, now that she has sent Estella away to a finishing school abroad).

Jaggers suggests they go back to Joe's, in order for him to explain the reason for his visit. He says that he feels his mission is ill-advised, but his client did not ask for his opinion; he is merely carrying out the instructions he is paid to follow. Firstly, he asks Joe if he will release Pip from his apprenticeship, without being paid compensation; naturally, Joe (like Biddy in the previous chapter) will not stand in Pip's way.

Jaggers then announces, in a business-like and matter-of- fact way, that Pip "has great expectations"; that he will "come into a handsome property" which his benefactor will give him; that he must immediately leave, to follow the way of life of a gentleman, and have a tutor; that he must still be referred to as "Pip"; and that the name of his benefactor is a secret to be revealed at some point in the future by that person, and one which must not be speculated on.

With hindsight, we understand why Jaggers is so vague about where and when the patron will be able to identify themselves to Pip "by word of mouth"; it is because Magwitch is barred from setting foot in England, and is living in New South Wales (Australia), that "It may be years hence".

After giving three opportunities for "objections" (rather like marriage banns), Jaggers, who now addresses Pip as "Mr Pip" (given his new status) but still conveys an air of "bullying suspicion", says that he already has money for Pip's "education and maintenance", and that he "must be better educated, in accordance with your altered position". He leaves twenty guineas to start with; Pip is to have new clothes made, and travel to London in a week's time, when he can stay with the tutor Matthew Pocket's son until his lessons start.

Because Pip knows that Matthew Pocket is a relative of Miss Havisham's, Jaggers' suggestion of him further reinforces the circumstantial evidence that the benefactor may be Miss Havisham.

Jaggers offers Joe compensation for terminating Pip's apprenticeship. Joe responds to the inference that he may see Pip in any commercial light with incoherent threats of violence, and refuses to take any of the money Jaggers has the power to give him. Jaggers retreats from the prospect of a physical fight, and takes the view that Pip cannot leave soon enough, "as you are to be a gentleman" and he thinks Joe is dangerous.

Joe and Biddy are sorry and sad that he will be leaving; Mrs Joe seems incapable of understanding what has been said, or its implications. For those who are staying, their composure soon returns; but Pip feels "quite gloomy…..I may have been, without quite knowing it, dissatisfied with myself".

Having told Biddy that his unhappiness stems from his inability to enter the gilded world of the gentleman, Pip's demand has been answered, as if by magic. Today's equivalent to Pip's dramatic change in circumstances would be a huge lottery jackpot win, and the question arising from that would be whether money (however you come by it) guarantees happiness. That is precisely the question Biddy had asked Pip in the previous chapter. In real life, when the dream suddenly comes true, adjusting to it suddenly seems more complicated than the lottery winner had ever imagined it would be.

Pip does not want to be seen in public in the village in his smart new clothes, because he thinks that would be "a coarse and common business", but he will show Joe and Biddy his outfit the evening before he leaves. The intervening time, they all say, echoing each other unconsciously, will (like Pip himself) "soon go".

Pip now sees his bedroom "as a mean little room that I should be parted from and raised above, for ever". He hopes that, in leaving it behind, he can resolve the conflict or "confused division of mind…..between the forge and Miss Havisham's, and Biddy and Estella". Pip feels that "this first night of my bright fortunes" is "the loneliest I had ever known". The subtext here is that the life he leaves is far simpler and less demanding than the metropolitan one he has been so keen to inhabit, and must now adapt to and live in. **Instead of being an apprentice blacksmith, he is an apprentice gentleman, and there is not the same supportive environment in which to learn his new occupation**; Jaggers is paid for what he does (as Pip's guardian), whereas Joe would never be. Jaggers thinks his instructions (from Magwitch) are ill-advised. He has no personal interest in Pip, but only a professional one.

This chapter could have a modern saying attached to it- **"be careful what you wish for". A fairy tale element has shot through Pip's life like a comet through the night sky. The obstacle which he has said is holding him back- his lack of** education and gentility- has disappeared with the spell cast by the magical words "great expectations".

Pip is now about 18 years old. Instead of (perhaps today) going to university, he is going to the university of life in London. **All the barriers to success, all the limitations of his background as a poor orphan, have been swept away. He does not have to go to London to seek his fortune, because he already has it. He has to discover, instead, whether the theory which has become so dear to him- that becoming a gentleman will make him happy- is true or not.**

Chapter 19

This is the last chapter of Dickens' first volume of the three which make up the novel. In terms of the overall length of the story, it is also a third of the way through; and the end of the chapter marks the point at which Pip is on the way to live in London and can no longer turn back**.**

Pip takes his leave of the marshes (not knowing that he will come back there); he remembers meeting Magwitch, and **experiences an ironic feeling of "comfort" at the notion that Magwitch may be dead (this affords a devastatingly neat contrast with the end of the second volume, in Chapter 39, where Pip is traumatised to find that Magwitch is very much alive).** He manages to start being condescending to both Joe and Biddy; he tells Biddy that he hopes "to remove Joe into a higher sphere" (of society), and so assumes that Joe, too, wants the social advancement which Pip has come to want so desperately for himself. Joe, of course, wants no such thing, because he is content with the life he has, and he has no pretensions, or expectations, of his own.

Biddy points out that Joe "may be proud", and may not wish to be removed from a place he is at home and comfortable with- a position in life which he accepts, without Pip's restless conviction that the grass is always greener on the other side of the hill. Pip is "disdainful", and he quite wrongly accuses Biddy of being "envious…grudging", and of showing "a bad side of human nature". She feels that Pip is being heartless and unjust; she is right. As a smaller child, Pip had felt injustice keenly, when he suffered it. He is less conscious of it when he is being less than generous towards Biddy.

Pip is becoming arrogant; he expects others, even those he knows well, to defer to him, and is disappointed that Joe is "so mightily secure of me". At the end of the previous chapter, "this first night of my bright fortunes" had been lonely; now, "the second night of my bright fortunes" is "as lonely and unsatisfactory as the first". But he cannot wait to go to London, for fear that it may have disappeared by the time he gets there, and, in the meantime, he has already developed an attitude to the villagers which Dickens summarises, memorably, as "a gallon of condescension" towards the "monotonous acquaintances of my childhood".

His patronising attitude to Joe is deeply ironic; he mentions to Biddy that Joe is "rather backward…..in his learning and his manners", but the same could be said of him, and **Herbert has to teach him proper table manners**. Pip already plans "to do something for Joe…..a rise in station", and he would like Biddy to continue to educate him in the meantime. Biddy points out that, precisely because of his lack of education, Joe will be happier where he is than he would be if he were removed "into a higher sphere". **Some people have already adjusted their expectations, to lead a happy life, without Pip's sense of restless dissatisfaction. Joe does not want for himself what Pip wants for him.**

The next morning, Pip visits the tailor Trabb to have his suit made. As soon as Pip mentions his fortune, Trabb's attitude changes; he becomes, if not exactly unctuous, very respectful and attentive, and addresses Pip as "Sir". The way people treat Pip with money is completely different from how they have treated him without it. Trabb's boy, who has been allowed to be as insolent as he liked until now, incurs Trabb's censure, and *Pip summarises the meeting as "my first decided experience of the stupendous power of money"*.

Pumblechook, too, is now friendly instead of patronising. He develops an uncontrolled passion for shaking Pip's hand; he feeds him the best meat, and addresses the chicken, saying it is fortunate to be on Pip's plate; a comical contrast with the childhood Christmas meal in Chapter 4, where Pip had been given "the scaly tip of the drumsticks of the fowls", and Pumblechook had implied that he deserved no better a fate than the Christmas pig.

Pumblechook now refers to Pip's harsh "bringing up by hand" as "the honour", as though Pip had been a distinguished visitor, not a troublesome encumbrance. Not only does he revise history, pretending that he had always treated Pip as his "chosen friend", and that he always knew Pip was "no common boy"; he asks Pip if he will put money into his seed business, to secure a local monopoly; all he needs is "More Capital", to enable "the realization of a vast fortune".

Both Trabb and Pumblechook find a new benevolence towards Pip which arises specifically from the fact that he can now help to make them richer; they are both traders, and both hypocrites.

Four days later, Pip dresses in his new clothes and goes to see Miss Havisham. Sarah Pocket's surprise at seeing him in his new finery does not lead Pip to question his assumption that Miss Havisham is his benefactor, or "the fairy godmother who had changed me". She does not defer to him, but still calls him "Pip", and speaks to him in the same way as before. She enjoys Sarah's envy, on the basis that Sarah, too, thinks that it is *Miss Havisham's* generosity to Pip- in preference to her own family- which has brought about this transformation for him. **Pip does not stop to ask himself what Miss Havisham means by saying that she has seen Jaggers and "heard about it"**; he thinks they are complicit in keeping her secret from Sarah.

Miss Havisham gloats, smiles cruelly at Sarah's "jealous dismay", and looks at her "with triumph in her weird eyes". **Her habitual enjoyment of other people's distress is a symptom of her unhealthy mind.**

Pip returns home for the last time, dresses up for Joe and Biddy, has a subdued meal with them, and leaves early in the morning. He is overcome with feelings of his own ingratitude, after Joe and Biddy throw old shoes after him for good luck; and he senses that the village had allowed him to be "innocent and little", while the "world spread before" him is "so unknown and great".

Reading this chapter, we share Pip's misgivings about his preparedness for this wide new world. However lacking in care and compassion the adults in his life have been, they have at least been consistent in their behaviour. Trabb and Pumblechook have started to flatter him and ingratiate themselves, in an attempt to exploit him and part him from his money; and Miss Havisham is equally exploitative and anti-social, in her own way. Pip's upbringing may have given him a high pain threshold, but it has not exposed him to the machinations of the adult world beyond his own village.

Summary - Chapters 14-19

Pip's time as Joe's apprentice had become as oppressive to him as a prison sentence, from the start, because he had felt as "flat and low" as the marshes. He is conscious only of "shame" about his home and surroundings, simply because Estella has been so contemptuous of Pip's "coarse and common" way of life.

Now that Satis House is out of bounds for him, Pip's thoughts are full of Estella and Miss Havisham. He is much keener to visit Estella again than, later, he is to see Joe. In agreeing to let Pip have time off to make that visit, Joe agrees to give Orlick the same courtesy. Orlick insults Mrs Joe; Joe fights him; and Orlick uses that evening to exact a cowardly revenge; he beats Mrs Joe senseless with a leg iron (the one Pip helped Magwitch to free himself from), and constructs an alibi of sorts, so that he escapes suspicion.

Biddy comes to look after the invalid Mrs Joe. While Pip is conscious that Biddy, who had always been dirty and shabby and down at heel, is now "bright and neat….clean….pleasant and wholesome and sweet-tempered" with eyes that are "curiously thoughtful and attentive…..very pretty and very good", he pays no regard to her merits, because he regards her as "common" (just as he is!!).

Biddy is smarter than Pip; wise and well balanced. She is open to admitting that she would regard Pip as "good enough" to marry, but she knows that she will not marry him, because Pip is obsessed with **Estella**'s beauty, and wants to become a gentleman in order to be worthy of her. Biddy points out that, if she will be so snobbish, she **is "not worth gaining over" (or having). Pip knows the truth of this, but will not accept it.**

Pip's frustration, because he will never have the financial means of becoming the gentleman he wants to be, **is swept away** when Jaggers comes to announce his "great expectations"; Pip is to take up the life of a gentleman in London immediately, and to be educated as such. With a fortune, Pip suddenly finds people like Pumblechook treating him respectfully. When Joe and Biddy are less inclined to flatter him, Pip is disappointed. Living in the great city appeals to him, as his future will be exciting, and he will be on equal terms with Estella. **He has too little appreciation of the value of the family he is leaving behind, and too little understanding that happiness and contentment have less to do with what you possess than with what you are.**

Pip stops being an apprentice blacksmith and becomes an apprentice gentleman, and an apprentice adult. At the age of about 18, he is escaping from the low prospects of his village; but will his great expectations of life in London be fulfilled, or disappointed?

The town where we find Satis House is modelled on Rochester in Kent- the birthplace of Dickens' mistress Ellen Ternan, for whom he had left his wife in 1858, three years before this novel was published. Dickens had first seen Ellen when she was aged 18, and acting at the Haymarket theatre in London. Perhaps Dickens had discussed with her how it felt to be a teenager moving to the big city; perhaps some of her hopes lie behind the thinking Dickens has given Pip in this part of his story.

Cast List and Chapter Locations – Book One

Use this handy checklist to save time and speed your revision. In particular, if you want to spend a session studying one particular character, use this list to find when – and the locations where - they appear.

Chapter 1   Pip, convict (Magwitch, unidentified)- churchyard

Chapter 2   Joe, Pip, Mrs Joe- home

Chapter 3   Pip, convicts (Compeyson, Magwitch, unidentified)- marshes

Chapter 4   Pip, Mrs Joe, Joe, Mr Wopsle, Mr & Mrs Hubble, Pumblechook, soldiers - home

Chapter 5   Soldiers, Mrs Joe, Pumblechook, Joe, Pip, Wopsle, two convicts- home and marshes

Chapter 6   Joe, Mrs Joe, Pip, Pumblechook, Wopsle- home

Chapter 7   Joe, Pip, then Pumblechook and Mrs Joe too- home

Chapter 8 Pumblechook, Pip, Estella, Miss Havisham- Pumblechook's shop and Satis House.

Chapter 9 Pumblechook, Mrs Joe, Pip, Joe- home

Chapter 10 Pip, Biddy and the "school"; Pip, Joe, Mr Wopsle and the "stranger" at the Three Jolly Bargemen; Pip, Joe and Mrs Joe at home

Chapter 11 Pip, Raymond, Camilla, Sarah Pocket, Georgiana, Estella, Jaggers (not yet identified), Miss Havisham, Herbert Pocket (not identified)- at Miss Havisham's

Chapter 12 Pip, Miss Havisham, Estella, Pumblechook, Joe, Mrs Joe- a summary of events over multiple visits to Satis House and at home

Chapter 13 Pip and Joe at Miss Havisham's; Pip, Joe, Mrs Joe and Pumblechook at Pumblechook's, the magistrates' court and the Blue Boar (with the Hubbles and Mr Wopsle)

Chapter 14 Pip- reflections on home- a chapter without action

Chapter 15 Pip and Joe at the Battery on the marshes; Pip, Joe, Orlick and Mrs Joe at the forge; Pip and Miss Havisham at her house; Pip, Mr Wopsle and Pumblechook at Pumblechook's; Pip, Mr Wopsle and Orlick walking home; Mrs Joe unconscious in her kitchen

Chapter 16 Pip, Joe, Mrs Joe, Orlick, Biddy, at home; several months pass, with Mrs Joe a housebound invalid; Biddy comes to live with them

Chapter 17 Pip and Biddy, at home and walking on the marshes; Orlick follows them home

Chapter 18 Pip, Joe, Wopsle, others and Jaggers at the pub; Pip, Joe, Biddy, Mrs Joe and Jaggers at home

Chapter 19 Joe, Biddy and Pip at home; Pip at Trabb's shop, Pumblechook's and Miss Havisham's; his final night at home and his departure in the early morning for London.

Book Two

Chapter 20

The journey to London takes five hours, and the world of London is very different from the slow, uncluttered one Pip comes there from.

As narrator, Pip, looking back, sees that London is "rather ugly, crooked, narrow, and dirty". Jaggers works round the corner from Smithfield market, a "shameful place, being all asmear with filth and fat and blood and foam". From here, Pip can see St Paul's Cathedral, but the view is obscured by "a grim stone building", Newgate Prison. Trials are ongoing, with "people standing about, smelling strongly of spirits and beer".

Dickens is interested in the dirt under the fingernails, and this chapter is full of **grubby characters with grubby clothes**- the coachman possesses "an old weather-stained pea-green hammercloth moth-eaten into rags"; **Mike** Spooney is "a gentleman with one eye, in a velveteen suit with a fur cap…who wiped his nose with his sleeve" who **is paid to find crooked witnesses to afford alibis to Jaggers' guilty defendants** . Pip is offered a front-row view of a trial (for an exorbitant price) by "an exceedingly dirty and partially drunk minister of justice", wearing "mildewed clothes", who shows him the gallows and the place where people are whipped in public. Pip's impression of the sights and smells is that London is "horrible…sickening". **There is a market in meat, a market in justice, and there is even a market in the clothes of the executed. Similarly, the "Jack", or odd-job man in chapter 54, recycles the clothes of those who have drowned and whose bodies have been washed up.**

Dickens lingers over the description of the lisping Jew, who is prepared to pay any price to have Jaggers represent his brother. The depiction of this man's anxiety, obsequiousness, and belief in the power of money seems like a caricature; it is pathetic and undignified. Jaggers will not abandon a client he has taken on, for any money, and treats the offer "with supreme indifference", because he is already engaged by the prosecution in this case. He is high-handed and curt with clients and potential clients; he shows a marked lack of empathy, and a marked focus on the task in hand.

He is completely unsentimental, and appears to see his profession as an occupation for money, with no higher purpose. He simply does what he is paid to do. He deploys emotion to motivate others to do what he wants them to. He will not be drawn into unnecessary discussion, because, as Wemmick says, "his time" is "valuable".

Jaggers' office is "a most dismal place" in "a gloomy street" called Little Britain; the wall opposite Jaggers' chair is "greasy with shoulders"; the office has a "dismal atmosphere", and has insects ("blacks and flies") in it.

Jaggers' character and professional reputation are established, while his actual appearance in this chapter is delayed, by what his clients and those who know him say about him. He inspires confidence and fear. When he does arrive, from court, he tells his clients not to think, because he is paid to do that for them. He concentrates on being paid, but his reputation as the lawyer to have on your side seems to be legendary.

Jaggers is an exceptionally organised man, who has attended in advance to the arrangements for Pip's accommodation and finances; he is to buy goods on credit, so that Jaggers can check his spending. Jaggers' office is tidier than Pip expects- "there were not so many papers about"- but it has an air of the unexplained, in the form of "some odd objects…..an old rusty pistol, a sword in a scabbard, several strange-looking boxes and packages", and, particularly, this-

"two dreadful casts on a shelf, of faces peculiarly swollen, and twitchy about the nose …I wondered whether the two swollen faces were of Mr Jaggers's family, and, if he were so unfortunate as to have had a pair of such ill-looking relations, why he stuck them on that dusty perch….instead of giving them a place at home".

These mysterious objects, together with the description of Jaggers' office chair, which is made "of deadly black horse-hair, with rows of brass nails round it, like a coffin", strike **a dark note.**

So this chapter gives us Pip's first experience of London. The coachman and the court officer try to extract money from him, for little or nothing; Jaggers' clients are a motley crew from the social underclass, unable to defend themselves and relying on him to protect them for money; the financial arrangements for Pip are prominent. Pragmatism rules, and none of these people have any great expectations. If Jaggers is "for you", you have good prospects of success at your trial; if he is against you, your case will be hopeless.

The cast of characters in this chapter is strikingly large; Pip, the coachman, the clerk (Wemmick, as yet unnamed), Spooney, a bystander, people standing about, the minister of justice, two men of secret appearance, a knot of three men and two women, a red-eyed little Jew and a second little Jew, Jaggers, the crooked witness ("murderous-looking", "guileless", "not by any means sober", and with a black eye), and another clerk. The total **is a minimum of eighteen, of whom only Pip is neither corrupt nor trying to purchase power through money**. Although **Jaggers** will not hear it said, we can see that he **has no scruples in finding corrupt witnesses; in the legal system, what you have done matters less than who you have on your side.**

Justice is a key concept, which Dickens threads all the way through the novel. Pip feels that the adults who abuse him when he is a small child are unjust ("there is nothing …..so finely felt, as injustice", Chapter 8). Estella is unjust. There will be no real justice for Magwitch, whose death saves him from execution for a victimless crime. Meanwhile, what Jaggers dispenses is malpractice and injustice too - Molly has escaped conviction, and he and Wemmick are careful to fix the evidence for their clients before they go to trial.

Jaggers wants to know as little as possible about anything which might compromise him. He would like to be high-minded, perhaps, but the murky practicalities of the law, and the fact that justice is never guaranteed, open up room for manoeuvre which he is skilled enough and pragmatic enough to take full advantage of. In London, money tends to gravitate from the weak to the powerful; poor value for money is to be had everywhere.

Pip is used to shaking hands in the village, even though Pumblechook takes the courtesy too far. **When Pip offers to shake Wemmick's hand, in the next chapter, Wemmick is suspicious, looking at Pip's hand "as if he thought I wanted something"**. This speaks volumes about the reserve and self-interest with which the people of London behave, and their knowingness contrasts with the naiveté of the people from the countryside.

Chapter 21

Wemmick walks Pip to the rooms at "Barnard's Inn" where he is to stay over the weekend with Herbert Pocket. Wemmick is "dry", "short" and "with a square wooden…block of a face" which lacks expressiveness. Pip thinks he is smiling, but he simply has "a post-office of a mouth", with "thin wide mottled lips"; his eyes are "small, keen and black…..glittering".

Wemmick's clothes are frayed, but he wears a lot of jewellery- "at least four mourning rings, besides a brooch representing a lady and a weeping willow at a tomb with an urn on it"; and his watch chain has attached to it "several rings and seals". Pip assumes that these mementoes indicate that he has suffered "a good many bereavements".

Wemmick's view of London is that, like anywhere else, "**you may get cheated, robbed, and murdered…… if there's anything to be got by it**". **Pip has always assumed that crimes are committed for a personal motive** ("If there is bad blood between you and them") and that the other type of crime- the opportunistic, or impersonal, is "worse"; Wemmick thinks they are both "much about the same". Pip is out of place in London because of his sense of moral relativism. **For Wemmick and Jaggers, the motive of the criminal is irrelevant; all that matters is collecting their fees, and then what can be done, by fair means or foul, to win the case.**

Pip finds that Barnard's Inn is not the hotel he thought it would be, but "the dingiest collection of shabby buildings ever squeezed together"; so dilapidated and decaying that Pip imagines the tenants kill themselves to escape the "most dismal" atmosphere.

He reflects **that this "realization of the first of my great expectations" is "so imperfect"**, and that "London was decidedly overrated". The narrative is grotesquely macabre- Pip thinks that the "melancholy little square" around which the decrepit buildings are grouped is "like a flat burying-ground", and that tenants who die in their rooms experience "unholy interment under the gravel". **Metaphorically, London is to be the graveyard of his expectations, just as the graveyard in the village in chapter one is where his brothers' hopes of economic success are buried with them.**

Pip recognises Herbert, as he reaches the top of the stairs, as "the pale young gentleman", before he recognises Pip as "the prowling boy". **The reappearance of Herbert, whose identity Pip has not known till now, prefigures Magwitch's unexpected return into Pip's life, at the place he lives in**; and both of them are to have an intimate financial relationship with him. Herbert's own furniture is only what "they could spare from home"; his room is "musty"; his father has no money to give him, and he would not take it if he had. **Herbert, like Pip used to be, is poor, away from his parents, and facing the task of making his way in the world alone.** That common ground underpins their friendship and leads Pip to support Herbert, financially, in secret.

Chapter 22

Herbert tells Pip that he, too, had been at Miss Havisham's because she had sent for him, "on a trial visit", "to see if she could take a fancy" to him. If she had, then he thinks she would have "provided for" him and that he would have been engaged to Estella. But he knows that Estella is "hard and haughty and capricious to the last degree, and has been brought up by Miss Havisham to wreak revenge on all the male sex". Herbert is realistic, just like Jaggers and Wemmick; Pip's view of the world (from outside London) is romanticised and naïve.

Herbert, being a relative of Miss Havisham's, knows that Jaggers is her "man of business and solicitor", and that he suggested that Matthew Pocket (Herbert's father) should be Pip's tutor. Just as Matthew "will not propitiate her", so his son has "a natural incapacity to do anything secret and mean".

Herbert decides to call Pip "Handel"; constructively corrects his mistakes in handling cutlery and glassware; and tells him Miss Havisham's story. Her mother died when she was a baby, and she was a spoilt child, and, like her father, she became "very rich and very proud". Her father remarried ("his cook, I rather think"), secretly, they had a son, and he only revealed the fact after the second wife had died. The boy "turned out riotous, extravagant, undutiful- altogether bad", and although his father relented from disinheriting him altogether, he left most of his money to his daughter, who was "a great match".

A man pursued Miss Havisham- "a showy-man, not to be...**mistaken for a gentleman**". But "she passionately loved him.....idolized him", and was "too haughty and too much in love, to be advised by anyone" and so he "got great sums of money from her, and he induced her to buy her brother out of a share in the brewery", so that once they were married he would run it. Herbert's father was the only person who told Miss Havisham that she "was doing too much for this man, and was placing herself too unreservedly in his power"; she would not listen, and they have not seen each other since.

Her fiancé then abandoned the wedding on the due day, writing her a letter; people thought that her half-brother was working with this confidence trickster, and shared the proceeds of the money he had induced Miss Havisham to give him. The two men fell into "deeper shame and degradation….and ruin" but Herbert does not know whether they are still alive.

Herbert's experience of being taken to Miss Havisham's for an unsuccessful "trial visit", the appointment of Jaggers as Pip's guardian, and the apparent success of Pip's ongoing contact with Miss Havisham, culminating in her meeting with Joe over the apprenticeship, lead both boys to suppose that, where Herbert failed, Pip succeeded. To the reader, Herbert's immunity to being spellbound by Estella seems reason enough for him to be discarded.

Herbert's version of **Miss Havisham's** story offers some motivation for her behaviour. A loveless childhood made her susceptible to being deceived, and she has been left with money instead of happiness, and with a monumental grudge. Why this should turn into a **desire for revenge on all men** is less convincing; but for her to try to make first Herbert (by association, a family enemy, as his father's son, whom Miss Havisham has disagreed with), and then Pip, fall for Estella **lends credence to Wemmick's assessment of misdeeds; they need not be motivated by a personal connection to the victim (Pip). You are just as likely to be robbed or cheated or killed by a stranger with no personal motive (Miss Havisham) as by someone you know who has a grudge against you (Orlick).**

Pip asks Herbert what he does for a living; he claims to be "an insurer of ships", and he has grandiose entrepreneurial plans to run a trading fleet. But there is no evidence of success or shipping connections where he lives. Pip finds out that Herbert has not, in fact, yet started work- he is merely "looking about me"- and he has no income. Just as he had persuaded himself that he had won his fight with Pip, so he has convinced himself that he has a successful career in business just around the corner- so much so that **Pip "began to think here were greater expectations than my own".**

Pip feels as though "it was many months" since he had left Joe and Biddy (it is actually three days), but "in the dusk of evening…. and in the dead of night" he feels bad about leaving them. While even the shambolic Barnard's Inn needs to be protected by "some incapable impostor of a porter", **the village** is a place of more modest proportions ("our old church" rather than Westminster Abbey) but where **people are less criminally inclined.**

On the Monday, as planned, Pip goes to Matthew Pocket's house, where he is to stay and study. Mrs Pocket has two nursemaids (Flopson and Millers) and seven small children at home, is absorbed in absent-minded reading about the born aristocracy, asks Pip how his mother is, and keeps dropping her handkerchief. She seems to have no interest in her children, who keep tripping up, and whom she sends indoors for a compulsory sleep in the middle of the afternoon. The rumpled appearance of Matthew Pocket, "with a rather perplexed expression of face, and with his very grey hair disordered on his head", indicates his lack of influence or control over his own family.

The airiness of the descriptions in this chapter should not distract us from a central point- **Matthew Pocket's shrewd analysis of gentlemanly qualities**. Miss Havisham's unscrupulous and low-born half-brother had felt "a deep and mortal grudge" against her, and so had conspired with Compeyson to ruin her. Compeyson was flamboyant ("a showy man"), but Matthew was insistent that he was no gentleman, although others were deceived into believing he was; and that she was "placing herself too unreservedly in his power". Matthew was the only "independent" member of her "scheming" family- he was "poor enough, but not time-serving or jealous". Miss Havisham accused him of being self-interested, and she ignored his advice- "she charged him…...with being disappointed in the hope of fawning upon her for his own advancement".

There is a remarkably close connection here with how Pip had treated Biddy in Chapter 19- accusing her of being "envious…and grudging….dissatisfied…..it's a bad side of human nature". Neither Miss Havisham nor Pip could recognise sound independent advice, because their own decision-making is too self-absorbed, and because they resent being challenged or criticised. **Where Compeyson was no gentleman (but a swindler), Matthew was a gentleman (and not a swindler), because he tried to protect Miss Havisham, with no intention of protecting any financial interest of his own. Pip learns to do just this when he tries to protect Magwitch in the final part of the novel.**

Herbert, like his father, is poor but gentlemanly, "frank and easy……(with) a natural incapacity to do anything secret and mean". Pip is struck by the fact that Herbert has great expectations but no way of starting his career; Pip knows that Herbert "would never be very successful or rich". This is "an odd impression" which returns later in the chapter. It leads Pip to his generous sponsorship of Herbert's job, later on. At the end of chapter 58, Pip concedes that he was wrong to think that Herbert demonstrated "inaptitude" for business.

When Miss Havisham dies, she has altered her Will, to recognise Matthew's value. His saying was that "no varnish can hide the grain of the wood"- that **true gentlemanliness can be distinguished** from the veneer of good manners, **by its lack of self-interest and its courage in speaking out when the truth has to be told.**

The idea of recognising value, and acknowledging it in words, is important. Magwitch verbalises to Pip the satisfaction he derives from their relationship, and Estella finally recognises the "worth" of Pip's attachment to her. Pip has to acknowledge the value, to him, of Joe and Biddy, before we can count him a real, grown-up gentleman.

Chapter 23

This chapter extends the description of the chaotic way of life in the Pocket household, and it includes the best joke in the novel.

Matthew Pocket is an educated man (Harrow and Cambridge) who finds himself in an anarchic family because his wife Belinda has no interest in her own children; she is distracted by her thwarted dreams of an aristocratic life, and grew up "guarded from the acquisition of plebeian domestic knowledge"……… "highly ornamental, but perfectly helpless and useless". **Her disappointed great expectations have come to nothing**, but have destroyed her potential to achieve anything or to be an effective parent or wife. Her life adds up to very little- she was "the object of a queer sort of respectful pity, because she had not married a title".

The joke reinforces Mrs Pocket's hopelessly wrong priorities. When a neighbour writes to her, alleging that Millers has been seen "slapping the baby", she makes no attempt to investigate, but, instead, she "burst into tears on receiving the note, and said that it was an extraordinary thing that neighbours couldn't mind their own business".

When Flopson hands her the baby, Mrs Pocket bangs its head on the table, by accident, while trying not to get its head stuck under the table; almost allows it to hurt itself severely with the nutcrackers; and tells off one of her still very young other children, Jane, for intervening because she is aware of the danger the baby is in. Mrs Pocket forgets she has the baby with her, because she is talking to Drummle about "two baronetcies".

Mrs Pocket is blind to the neglectful behaviour of the servants, and obsessed with the idea of her own status. The cook has realised that, simply by telling Mrs Pocket that "she felt I was born to be a Duchess", she can be immune to criticism, and can then behave however she likes. The house is run by the servants, for the benefit and comfort of the servants.

At moments of silent frustration (or "desolate desperation"), Mr Pocket has a habit of pulling his hair and trying to lift himself up into the air. Pip did something similar in Chapter 17, when he could not express his feelings about Estella to Biddy ("I.....got a good grasp on the hair on each side of my head, and wrenched it well"). He has the same openness and smile as Herbert, is "unaffected" (i.e. he has no pretentious mannerisms), and his distress at the domestic chaos around him is presented as comic. We feel sorry for him; **his expectations of a career in law or the church have evaporated**, and he seems to have settled for second best in his professional and family life; he is truly like Herbert, in that he will never be very successful or rich, because he simply does not have the capacity to be either. But Matthew's merit finally leads Miss Havisham to revise her opinion of him, on Pip's insistence; she leaves him £4000 when she dies.

The house is run by the servants, whom Mrs Pocket refuses to control- Pip suspects that the best food and entertainment is to be found "down stairs". Mr Pocket works hard, teaching, editing and proofreading, and scrapes together enough money to keep the expensive façade of a household running. The cook "had mislaid the beef", and is later found "insensibly drunk on the kitchen floor"; Flopson and Millers leave the children with their parents (inadequate babysitters) when they have "some private engagement"- a comic inversion of the employer-employee relationship. Mrs Pocket's refusal to challenge or manage the servants promotes "a smooth way of going on" in that there is no "trouble" or conflict; but the lack of structure or organisation explains the initial sight Pip had of the children of the family "in various stages of tumbling up".

Pip has two fellow-students staying at the Pockets'- Startop and Drummle. They each have a boat, and in the evenings they row on the river Thames at the bottom of the garden. Pip wants to be competitive and to be better than them, and takes lessons in rowing so that he has "elegance of style for the Thames"

A good deal of care and time is taken over the description of **Drummle**, starting here and building in the next few chapters. He **is from an aristocratic background, but is boorish and unintelligent- a kind of metropolitan Orlick**. He is "an old-looking young man of a heavy order of architecture", "sulky" and uncommunicative- but he is "actually the next heir but one to a baronetcy…he spoke as one of the elect". Drummle is important because he will go on to marry Estella, and, in order for us to share Pip's appalled shock when he finds that out, our low opinion of Drummle has to be formed early in the narrative.

Pip meets the Pockets' "toady neighbour", Mrs Coiler, who, true to her name, is like a snake- insinuating, "serpentine…..altogether snaky and fork-tongued". Rather like the Jew in Chapter 20, she seems an irrelevant character, introduced arbitrarily, and discarded without any development.

It is interesting that where Dickens tries to be entertaining and light in tone- as in this chapter- the effect does not translate very well to us reading him a hundred and fifty years later. The humour seems clumsy and rather laboured, and the style is overwritten for modern taste.

We are laughing unsympathetically at Mrs Pocket, and we feel a little guilty for doing so; we feel sorry for the children, who are verbally abused, and neglected, by their own mother. Perhaps we feel that what Dickens chooses as his subject matter for humour is not always appropriate or comfortable. When the comedy is in the writing- when it is presented through observation and language, rather than dramatically- we find it more enjoyable and entertaining.

The more successful aspects of Dickens' comic writing here are the foibles and character he gives to Mr and Mrs Pocket; his pulling of his hair, and her distracted behaviour, and the way she asks irrelevant questions, because her mind is on the aristocratic life she wishes she could have had. These elements are reminiscent of Jane Austen, and they do amuse us. We are less satisfied by the caricatures of Mrs Coiler and the drunk cook, and we find it frustrating that the seven small children should be exposed to the lack of care of their nursemaids and the benign neglect of their parents.

We are conditioned to expect our novels- like our television dramas or feature films- to be driven by plot, so we become frustrated quite quickly when the plot does not seem to be moving forward. Dickens was writing in a different tradition, where the protagonist's experiences could legitimately be explored at length as part of their life story; the process of their journey to maturity could be a leisurely one. It is not for nothing that this book has 450 pages! Were the same plot to be written today, we would expect it all to be wrapped up in less than 100,000 words or 300 pages. If we ever become frustrated with Dickens' style, it is when he tries to write humorously, but our frustration is the product of changing cultural tastes, not a lack of skill on his part.

Thus far, **Dickens has kept the plot tense, by leaving the reader seeking answers to half-hidden questions.**

Now, the main question is <u>whether Miss Havisham is indeed Pip's benefactor</u>, so we tend, with our expectations of narrative, to be less appreciative of any episode which does not contribute to the main thrust of the plot. We need to remember that Dickens felt he had written a considerably comic novel, and that it is not his fault that the passing of time has been less kind to his taste in humour than to his extraordinarily clever control over complexity and the structure of the novel.

Chapter 24

Pip agrees with Matthew Pocket's definition of the education he is to have. It is intended to enable him not to be out of place among "the average of young men in prosperous circumstances" (later, we understand why- **Magwitch wants to make a gentleman**, and as he does not have any education himself, he wants Pip to have more, yet without the need for anything academic) . It will not be demanding, so Pip wants to keep his second home with Herbert and buy the furniture there, which has been rented. As this will save Herbert money, Matthew insists that Jaggers must approve it; so Pip visits him at his office, and the rest of the chapter deepens our understanding of Jaggers' authority and his foibles.

The way he negotiates with Pip the sum of money he needs for the furniture is "strongly marked…and not of an agreeable kind" (it also echoes the mental arithmetic exercises Pumblechook imposed on Pip in Chapter 8). Jaggers does not laugh, ever, but his boots "creak, as if they laughed in a dry and suspicious way". Wemmick says that Jaggers is highly skilled, successful in his business, and as "deep as Australia", and that he likes to make the people he deals with feel that they do not understand his way of handling them- this is "professional: only professional".

Wemmick says that Jaggers seems to him to behave as though he has "set a mantrap and was watching it. Suddenly-click-you're caught!". He shows Pip the rest of the office, which is "dark and shabby", and the three clerks who work there, with clients who are "shabby" or "with weak eyes".

Pip raises the issue of the identity of "the two odious casts with the twitchy leer". Wemmick explains that these **are death-masks of two criminals just after they have been executed**- one was a murderer, and the other was a forger of Wills, and a possible murderer. Both of these men- and other clients also- had sent for the mourning-rings and trinkets which Wemmick wears as part of his work clothes. He accepts them because they are "curiosities", and, though not valuable, they are "portable property", which Wemmick, in the absence of what he calls Pip's "brilliant look-out" (or outlook/prospects), never misses an opportunity to accumulate.

Wemmick invites Pip to stay overnight at his house at Walworth, where there are more "curiosities". He tells Pip that Jaggers will invite him to dinner, and that **Pip should "look at his housekeeper" who is "a wild beast tamed"**, because it will raise further his appreciation of Jaggers' abilities. This is an allusion to Jaggers' spectacular success at the start of his legal career, in having Molly, now his housekeeper, found innocent of a murder she had committed, because of the arguments he used at the trial.

Finally, Wemmick invites Pip to watch Jaggers in action; he is in court, "striking…..everybody present with awe". He makes people shiver, or hang on his words "in dread rapture", or shrink under his close attention. **Jaggers shares a taste**

for the theatrical with Mr Wopsle, but Jaggers is a professional, and what is at stake is life and death, not entertainment.

This chapter confirms and extends some of what we already know about Jaggers; he is a master of psychology and of exploiting other people's weakness. His clients are invariably weak and desperate. The mementoes which he and Wemmick keep are macabre, and neither man seems emotionally involved in the least with those who have passed through their offices.

What emerges is a picture of **the class system in London. There is a criminal underclass (Jaggers' clients); a corrupt underclass of servants at the Pockets' (and elsewhere); a working class (Matthew Pocket, Herbert Pocket, Wemmick and his fellow clerks); an idle class (Pip, Drummle, Startop, Mrs Coiler, Belinda Pocket); and a professional class (Jaggers). Money flows from one to another, and there is a striking absence of any sense that, as a member of this society, you are responsible in any way for anyone else.**

In Chapter 20, Pip/Dickens commented that "We Britons" had decided that we had and were "the best of everything"- that our way of life was enterprising and progressive. Pip (Dickens) sees that life in London, close up, looks "rather ugly, crooked, narrow, and dirty". **Pip's dead brothers, in Chapter 1, had given up "trying to get a living, exceedingly early in that universal struggle". In these London chapters, Dickens is showing us that struggle to earn a living, and how the struggle deadens feelings of compassion** – the feeling of "a sublime compassion for the poor creatures who were destined" to go to Pip's village church every Sunday, make nothing of their lives, and then be buried, "to lie obscurely at last among the low green mounds" (Chapter 19).

Perhaps Dickens intends us to note that, while we live in what we know as "Great Britain", Jaggers' office is in "Little Britain". The nation, its aspirations and its sophistication are all smaller than we might be inclined to admit, when we see it closely, at first hand.

Chapter 25

The description of Drummle is repeated and developed ("sulky….Heavy in figure, movement, and comprehension…sluggish…the large awkward tongue that seemed to loll about in his mouth…idle, proud, niggardly, reserved, and suspicious…a blockhead"). He is hardly a positive advertisement for the English aristocracy.

Pip and Startop (who "had been spoilt by a weak mother") can row much better than Drummle, but Pip's real "intimate companion and friend" is Herbert.

After "a month or two", Matthew's sister- Camilla- and Georgiana pay a visit to the Pockets. This takes us back to Chapter 11, where Camilla had been critical of Matthew for failing to dress his children "in the deepest of trimmings to their mourning" at a funeral, and had made a fool of herself by claiming that her symptoms of physical illness were due to her extreme devotion and concern for Miss Havisham.

We already think of Camilla as utterly insincere. Now, she and Georgiana, perceiving that Miss Havisham has preferred Pip to them, "hated me with the hatred of cupidity and disappointment"- because his arrival seems to have deprived them of their own great expectations. **It is not just Matthew and Herbert, but the rest of Miss Havisham's relatives, who think she has chosen to become Pip's benefactor**, and so disposed of her wealth outside the family. Camilla is motivated by greed; it is not just having money which is dangerous, but the desire for money; Pip did not deserve their hatred before he had a benefactor, and he does not deserve it now.

Most of this chapter is taken up by Pip's visit to Wemmick's home. Wemmick tells Pip that Jaggers never locks his windows or doors, because there is no criminal who would dare burgle him and face him in court; they fear him. At the same time, Jaggers takes the precaution of having nothing valuable in his home; the spoons look silver, but are made of "Britannia metal". Jaggers therefore knows the value of money and caution (which equips him to be Pip's "guardian") but he also relishes conflict, and winning (Wemmick's concept of his setting a "mantrap"- "He'd have their lives….He'd have all he could get…..it's impossible to say what he couldn't get, if he put his mind to it").

Wemmick lives in a tiny wooden cottage with a garden (rather like Joe's small wooden house). He has lavished care on it, with the drawbridge, the flagpole, and the cannon which he fires at 9 p.m. every day, the complicated paths, the ornamental lake; it is a miniature castle. He keeps a strict distinction between his life at work and his life at home, and **looks after his father**, the "aged parent" ("a very old man in a flannel coat: clean, cheerful, comfortable, and well cared for, but intensely deaf") **dutifully and with enthusiasm**.

It has taken years for Wemmick "to bring the property up to its present pitch of perfection" and to buy it, bit by bit. It may not be portable, but it is property; Wemmick has no children of his own, and no-one to pass it on to. His father says that it "should be kept together by the Nation, after my son's time".

The "curiosities" which Wemmick had promised to show Pip are all to do with crime, including **"several manuscript confessions written under condemnation", which Wemmick stresses are lies (thy could, of course, be true).** Pip enjoys the food, and the only drawback is that he is sleeping so close under the roof that it is as if the flagpole were resting on his forehead. It is a "crazy little box of a cottage", but Wemmick refers to it as "the Castle". It is an outlet for his creativity and emotional energy.

As they walk back to the office the next morning, Wemmick's expression becomes "dryer and harder" as he adopts his work persona, so that he can present a tone of professional detachment. This tension between work and home, between behaving as you feel and as your job requires you to, is one which Pip never had to deal with at Joe's forge.

Wemmick's elaborate construction of a drawbridge (a plank) and a moat (two feet deep) is rather like Jaggers' hand-washing. It creates a sense of separation and sanctuary from the compromises and moral battles of their daily work. **Wemmick** is like Joe, in that he is a creature of habit. His **only expectation is to marry Miss Skiffins, which he does**. Even his practical sense and hard-headedness (and he is habitually described as wooden) is not enough to detect Compeyson's deceit. It is Wemmick who gives Pip the signal to move Magwitch. When Magwitch is caught, Wemmick is unemotional about his fate, but animated about the opportunity to secure his "portable property".

Chapter 26

Jaggers, too, has Pip (and Herbert, Startop and Drummle) to dinner at his house. This chapter raises **two mysteries; why does Jaggers take such an interest in Drummle, and what is the significance of his maid Molly and the strength she has in her wrists?**

There is more about Jaggers' hand-washing, which seems to be some sort of compulsion. Every time he returns from court or finishes seeing a client, he washes his hands thoroughly. When he is walking home with Pip, he ignores people who recognise him in the streets.

His home is in Gerrard Street, in Soho, and it needs painting and has dirty windows. He only uses part of it, "three dark brown rooms on the first floor", "up a dark brown staircase". The "carved garlands on the panelled walls" remind Pip of nooses. The best room is full of legal books, and "there was nothing ornamental to be seen", because Jaggers, unlike Wemmick, is one-dimensional, and interested only in his work. There is nothing in Jaggers' home which expresses his personality, because his professional life is all there is of him.

Jaggers hands out clean cutlery and plates after every course of the meal, and "kept everything under his own hand, and distributed everything himself". His controlling behaviour extends to how he speaks to Molly and the absolute way he insists that she shows the boys her wrists. He is arbitrary and firm in declaring that the evening ends at 9.30 pm. No-one challenges or stands up to Jaggers. He goes on to "screw discourse" or conversation out of Drummle

He immediately labels Drummle as "the Spider", because he is "blotchy, sprawly, sulky", and declares "I like the look of the fellow". Later, his response to Startop is "coarse" and "lumpish" and Jaggers has to intervene to stop Drummle from throwing a glass at Startop's head. Despite this violent and oafish behaviour, Jaggers tells Pip, afterwards, "I like that Spider though", because "he is one of the true sort", although Pip should keep away from him as far as possible. He even starts to predict what will happen to Drummle, but checks himself ("Why, if I was a fortune-teller.................But I am not a fortune-teller"). The chapter ends with the information that, about a month later, Drummle's time at the Pockets' ends, "and, to the great relief of all the house but Mrs Pocket, he went home to the family hole". Pip had described him as a creeping amphibian in Chapter 25.

There is nothing civilised or genteel about Drummle; he is an anti-social, inarticulate, unintelligent thug (very much like Orlick). He does not deserve Jaggers' favourable opinion of him, and, because Jaggers is successful in a profession which demands good judgment of people, we wonder even more at what seems a lack of judgment and insight on his part here. At this point in the novel, we have no clue to Drummle's significance; with hindsight, we have to conclude that Jaggers has instructions from Miss Havisham to find an object like Drummle for Estella to torment, or, perhaps- as happens- to be married to.

He seems to see Drummle as a match for Estella, and has considered the implications of it, because he talks to Pip about the power struggle they will have, in Chapter 48. It is notable that Startop has only a walk-on part in this chapter or scene, and we scarcely know that Herbert is even there.

The housekeeper, Molly, is a striking and disturbing figure. Twice, Pip says that her appearance- "extremely pale, with large faded eyes, and a quantity of streaming hair………lips….parted…as if she were panting…..her face looked to me as if it were all disturbed by fiery air" reminds him of "the faces I had seen rise out of the Witches' caldron" in "Macbeth". Wemmick had already told Pip to look out for her, as she is "a wild beast tamed". He senses that there is an odd tension in her relationship with Jaggers; she does not want him to call her back, after she has put a dish on the table, "and wanted him to speak when she was nigh, if he had anything to say". He seems to Pip to be keeping her in an artificial state of nervous suspense.

Jaggers is watching Drummle with a degree of interest which Pip finds "quite inexplicable", and Molly is clearing the table, when Jaggers suddenly "clapped his large hand on the housekeeper's, like a trap" (Wemmick had used the term "mantrap", you will remember), and tells her to "let them see your wrist". Molly is hiding her other hand behind her back; she begs Jaggers not to force her to do this, but he has "an immovable determination", so she has to obey. The wrist she was hiding is "much disfigured- deeply scarred and scarred across and across".Jaggers talks about the "power of wrist… force of grip" in Molly's hands, while he is "coolly tracing out the sinews with his forefinger". **We have no idea why this is important; all we can do is put it aside as a new mysterious point to be explained later.**

The sense of something unnatural or even supernatural is reinforced by this very strange and unexplained sentence-

"Years afterwards, I made a dreadful likeness of that woman, by causing a face that had no other natural resemblance to it than it derived from flowing air, to pass behind a bowl of flaming spirits in a dark room".

Jaggers controls the conversation, too, and Pip recognises that "he wrenched the weakest part of our dispositions out of us". Pip "boasts of my great prospects" and his "tendency to lavish expenditure", but it is Drummle who emerges in the worst light. When the others talk about Drummle's slowness at rowing on the river, he claims to be stronger and more skilful; Jaggers has "wound him up to a pitch little short of ferocity", and Drummle is "sulky…morose…offensive…surly" and his "obtuseness" becomes "intolerable".

The boys have had too much to drink and they take exception to Drummle's "boorish sneer…..that we were too free with our money"; Pip points out that Drummle has himself recently borrowed money from Startop. Drummle despises the other boys, and, when Startop makes a joke at his expense, he becomes violent; he will not forget or forgive, and walks home on the other side of the road from Startop.

Pip goes back to apologise to Jaggers for "anything disagreeable"; Jaggers has not been offended in any way- in truth, because he has "screwed" and "wrenched" the conversation to the point of tension and conflict. He has demonstrated his mastery over Molly (she calls him "Master"); he has observed the weakness of Pip and the company he keeps; and he has, for some strange reason, taken a liking to Drummle.

Summary - Chapters 20-26

The setting of the novel moves to London, and we tour a number of locations- Little Britain and its surroundings, and the homes of Wemmick, Jaggers, Matthew Pocket, and Pip and Herbert. The descriptions here are as detailed as those of Pip's home at the forge and of Satis House, and more detailed than the descriptions of Pumblechook's or the Three Jolly Bargemen.

For the narrative to be convincing, it is important that it is not just Pip who believes that his benefactor is Miss Havisham. Pumblechook and the "toadies" in Miss Havisham's family find it convenient to believe it. Joe, Pip and Herbert cannot reasonably be expected to think otherwise. Jaggers and Wemmick know the truth, but cannot disclose it.

The dramatic momentum which drives the rest of the novel forward depends on us knowing more or less the same as Pip. Sometimes, we feel we know more than he does; but **if the novel had an omniscient narrator it would have little or no suspense** (we would know what Orlick and Compeyson were doing, and we would know that Pip's fortune comes from Magwitch, not Miss Havisham).

The disturbing representation of Molly- as someone who might have emerged from the witches' cauldron in "Macbeth"- plays up this strand of hidden secrets, or non-disclosure, which is new to Pip. **It is only in London that secrecy reigns**; life in the village is more straightforward. It is only in London that we find Wemmick's double life, and the absolute distinction (Jaggers has it too) between the "professional" and the "personal". Jaggers is developed as a terrifying and commanding figure, although he seems to have no real personal life at all. He is "deep as Australia"- unfathomable; bloodthirsty, in the sense that he would "have the lives" of as many people who might try to rob him; and he could achieve anything he sets his mind to.

The use and abuse of power is starting to emerge in these chapters as **a major theme**. The servants run the Pockets' house. Miss Havisham and Jaggers both exercise a high level of control, over Estella and Molly, respectively. Wemmick has his domestic life settled and ordered to the smallest degree.

Those who fall foul of the legal system, by contrast, **have no power** over their lives. Jaggers' clients and would-be clients are taking part in a glorified lottery. He is not interested in what they think; he does their thinking for them. The substance of the law matters less than who is representing you; **Jaggers and Wemmick construct**

the "evidence" to serve their clients' case. When, much later, Jaggers tells Pip that he would not have been mistaken about the source of his expectations if he had concentrated on the evidence, he is being harsh; **Jaggers himself manipulates evidence** whenever it suits him, and built his professional career on the stage management of Molly's trial- not on the facts.

Dickens has prepared the ground in these chapters for **the empathy** he shows **with the condemned criminal**. One of the first sights of London Pip has is of the door from which **four debtors will emerge "to be killed in a row" (Chapter 20)- this links with the description of the condemned colonel (Chapter 32) and the court scene in Chapter 56. Dickens writes about the plight of those condemned to death with particular sensitivity.**

Chapter 27

Biddy writes to Pip, saying that Joe and Mr Wopsle are coming to London. Her letter uses the more formal salutation "Mr Pip"; she hopes that Pip will see Joe "for the love of poor old days…I hope…it will be agreeable to see him even though a gentleman…he is a worthy worthy man".

Pip feels not "pleasure" at the thought of seeing Joe, but "considerable disturbance, some mortification, and a keen sense of incongruity"; he would pay to keep Joe away, and particularly wants him not to meet Drummle. This tells us that Pip is uncomfortable at the thought that his old ties will disturb his old emotions, and, perhaps, his new connections; he would like to evade them, but **even money cannot be used to protect us from our capacity for feeling and for guilt**.

Pip's extravagance means he is constantly decorating the rooms at Barnard's Inn, expensively, and "in some quite unnecessary and inappropriate way", and he has employed a manservant, a boy called Pepper, a "monster" whom Pip has to feed and find work for, and whom he describes as "this avenging phantom".

The meeting, over breakfast, gives Dickens the opportunity to write another comic scene. Joe is clumsy, his speech has an accentuated countriness here, and his hat keeps falling off the mantel-piece. Wopsle has left the employment of the Church and is trying to become a professional in "the playacting". Joe starts calling Pip "Sir" and he feels socially uncomfortable and "stiff" when he meets Herbert. His feeling awkward means that he coughs a great deal, "and dropped so much more than he ate, and pretended that he hadn't dropped it". Pip "had neither the good sense nor the good feeling to realise that this was all my fault", and that he has failed to make Joe feel relaxed.

When Herbert goes to work, Pip still has to ask Joe to be less formal. Joe intends "to stay not many minutes more"; his "only wish" is "to be useful to" Pip. He explains that Pumblechook is claiming that he had brought Pip up, and had told Joe that Miss Havisham wanted to see him; and Miss Havisham wants Joe to pass on to Pip the message that **"Estella has come home and would be glad to see him"**.

Biddy refused to put that message into a letter, and insisted instead that Joe should come and tell Pip the news himself. Joe will not stay in London a moment more than he has to, because he feels out of place, anywhere except in "the forge, the kitchen, or…th' meshes". Touchingly, Joe feels that he is "awful dull". He harbours no resentment of Pip and the different path their lives have taken, because "life is made of ever so many partings welded together". Pip, like us, is struck by Joe's "simple dignity".

Pip would rather not think about Joe, Biddy and his sister, because he feels he has let them down, by leaving them and not expressing his gratitude; he has underappreciated what they have done for him. But the reappearance of Estella is bound to arouse his interest and curiosity, and to suppress those feelings.

Joe is clumsy in his speech and movement. The fact that he can barely read or write means that it is hard for him to read the nameplates at Barnard's Inn, and he thinks that "Havisham" begins with the letter A. Pip would be ashamed to let Drummle see him. But **Joe is gentlemanly in that he comes to London, despite his discomfort and feeling out of place, in order to do an old friend a service and deliver the message about Estella**. Pip, by contrast, is conscious of his own "weaknesses and meannesses", and of his failure to make feel Joe feel relaxed- he feels impatient and cross with Joe instead.

Joe draws a dignified end to his old relationship with Pip, in his speech at the end of the chapter. It is not the physical distance between the marshes and London that matters, but the two worlds are alien to each other. If Wemmick cannot integrate his Walworth life and his Little Britain one, Pip will be unable to balance his life as a London gentleman with his past. Joe realises that Pip, still at only age 19 or so, has taken an irreversible step away from his past and his old friends.

Chapter 28

Pip decides that he "must" go to Miss Havisham's the next day. As readers, we do not see the urgency; it indicates that there is not enough going on in Pip's life- he has no profession and too much leisure.

He feels sorry about his behaviour to Joe, and first thinks he should stay at Joe's, in a spirit of "repentance", but then he starts "to invent reasons and make excuses" to stay at the Blue Boar in the town instead. Looking back, he knows that he is deluding himself, in that his real motive is that he wants to see Estella sooner than he wants to try to improve his relationship with Joe and Biddy.

Pip feels uncomfortable about taking his servant with him because he thinks he would be out of place among the people Pip knows from his days in poverty- and that "the Avenger" and Trabb's boy might find ways of humiliating him.

There are two convicts being taken on the coach on their way to the prison ship. The "taller and stouter" of the two is recognisable as the stranger who gave Pip the two pound notes on Magwitch's behalf, because of his "half-closed eye" (see Chapter 10). He does not recognise Pip because of the change in his appearance (over several years, "in the course of nature") and clothes. Pip half-dreams about giving the two pounds back, and when he wakes up the convicts are discussing the two one pound notes he had delivered, and the donor is identified as Magwitch. Although he did not know the convict with the half-closed eye, who was being freed from prison ("different gangs and different ships"), Magwitch asked him to find "that boy that had fed him and **kept his secret**" and give him the money. Since then, Magwitch has been "tried again for prison breaking, and got made a Lifer".

Pip gets off the coach early, and walks the rest of the way. He has an "undefined and vague" fear, "a dread", which "made me tremble", as he remembers "the terror of childhood", the encounter with Magwitch in the churchyard and the threats Magwitch made (Chapter 1).

The chapter ends on a lighter note. Pip is recognised by the waiter at the Blue Boar, who shows him an old article in the local newspaper, which reported (without referring to him by name) Pip's "recent romantic rise in fortune", and claimed that Pumblechook had been his "earliest patron, companion, and friend". Pip feels that even if he went to the North Pole, some Eskimo would have heard that Pumblechook had been his childhood guide, so ruthless has Pumblechook's self-promotion been. This theme recurs in chapter 58.

The narrative includes the outraged reaction of a "choleric gentleman" to having to travel on the coach with a pair of convicts; he is in the chapter purely to **satirise stereotypical reactions to the convicted**. It is notable that, although Mrs Joe says that "people are put in the Hulks because they murder....rob...forge......and do all sorts of bad", **Dickens never tells us what these convicts, or Magwitch, have done**.

Even Jaggers perverts the course of justice; even Estella is the daughter of a convict and a murderess; our pretensions to gentility or superiority may well be without any real foundation; and so we should not be judgmental about other people, because, as Joe says to Magwitch, at the end of Chapter 5, "we don't know what you've done, but we wouldn't have you starved to death for it, poor miserable fellow-creatur". The labels "law-abiding" and "criminal" can be as inexact and misleading as the labels "common" and "gentleman".

Chapter 29

This is an important chapter, positioned almost exactly half way through the novel. **Pip/Dickens tries to explain Pip's fascination with Estella**; the whole ethos of the place of Miss Havisham and Estella in Pip's life is one he regards as **a romantic fairy tale** in which he is the prince who rides to the rescue of the damsel, puts Satis House back into the light and the normal world, and marries Estella ("the Princess"). But we (with the benefit of Pip's own hindsight) see it as a grotesque nightmare of heartlessness on the part of these two women.

Pip himself, in hindsight, sees himself here as a "wretched boy", because, **in his quest for gentility, he has left behind what was good and loyal in his upbringing and entered a world of calculated exploitation**. The vulnerable and the outcast- Pip, Magwitch, and the criminals whom Jaggers defends with varying success, and from whom Wemmick takes their "portable property"- are the victims of heartlessness on the part of those who have power over them. All that differentiates the unsentimental heartlessness of Jaggers and Wemmick from that of Miss Havisham and Estella is the fact that it is to do with money rather than emotion.

It is a natural and understandable mistake for Pip to assume that Miss Havisham is his benefactor; he cannot be expected, yet, to realise that there is no "evidence" (as Jaggers puts it) to prove it. The past circumstances- Miss Havisham's bizarre and unexplained summons, the circumstantial meeting with Jaggers there on the stairs, the way in which Miss Havisham takes Pip into her confidence, and her acknowledged wealth- all point in that direction. Pip has grown up previously only with the straightforward roughness of Mrs Joe, and the simple goodness of Biddy; **he has had no prior experience of manipulative, devious feminine behaviour.**

Pip's visit reinforces his sense of shame over Joe- he is ashamed of himself, for again failing to visit him, and he is ashamed of Joe, because Estella is still so critical of anyone coarse or common- "naturally…what was fit company for you once, would be quite unfit company for you now". His intention is to see Joe the next day, but, instead, he goes back to London with Jaggers by coach, because Estella's snobbishness, and his infatuation with her, makes the thought of seeing Joe as hurtful as the thought of not seeing him- she would disapprove. In her presence, he feels coarse and common, even though, as he points out in the narrative, he is wearing "lighter boots than of yore".

Pip's obsession with Estella is such that he feels he is "set apart for her and assigned to her". This is adolescent wish-fulfilment. It grips Pip's imagination, so that he walks about "painting brilliant pictures of her plans" for him. He has convinced himself that because Miss Havisham "had adopted Estella, and had as good as adopted me, it could not fail to be her intention to bring us together"- **we can see the faulty logic here quite clearly.**

Pip the adult narrator can see that his "life and character" are "boyish", which allows Estella to take "such strong possession of me"; that he is walking into an insoluble problem, "a poor labyrinth" from which he will be unable to extricate himself, because, stripped of the romantic imagination, his love for her, which is fixed, "once for all", because he finds her "irresistible", is at the same time "against reason, against promise, against peace, against hope, against happiness, against all discouragement". The difference between truth and illusion is important, but it comes from judgment, not from education or wealth. **Pip is under a spell; Estella looks "more bright and beautiful than before", and so he is "under stronger enchantment" than he was before Estella's recent phase of growing up and growing more beautiful in France.**

His expectations of Estella are both great, and highly romantic. At the beginning of the previous chapter, Pip (as narrator) has told us about his capacity to deceive himself about his own motivation. Here, **he deludes himself by convincing himself**

that what he wants to happen must, logically, happen. It is not true that because Miss Havisham has adopted Estella, and has "as good as" adopted him, "it could not fail to be her intention to bring us together".

Estella behaves as she always has. She says she has no recollection of those moments which mean so much to Pip; she is "cold and careless", "haughty", and has an air of "completeness and superiority". As her beauty has increased ("so much more beautiful, so much more womanly"), Pip feels she is unattainable ("the sense of distance and disparity….the inaccessibility"), and is conscious all over again of his being a "coarse and common boy".

It is to the hold over him that Estella has that Pip attaches "**all those wretched hankerings after money and gentility that had disturbed my boyhood**", his sense of shame, and "the innermost life of my life". The description, again, of "her face in the glowing fire…….to look in at the wooden window of the forge and flit away" is reminiscent of Cathy at Heathcliff's window in Emily Bronte's famous novel, "Wuthering Heights"- a symbol of Romantic/Gothic obsession.

As they walk in the garden, which is "too overgrown and rank for walking in with ease", Estella influences Pip to adopt the same supercilious and "condescending" attitude she has towards Joe, and, more generally, to "what was fit company for you once". Perhaps the garden- where Pip sees not the reality of weeds in the cracks in the wall, but, in his imagination, "the most precious flowers that ever blew"- is a dysfunctional, decayed version of the Garden of Eden he would like to walk in with Estella. Shakespeare, too, uses the word "rank", and the imagery of weeds and gardens more darkly, throughout "Hamlet", to convey the sense that something is profoundly wrong, and that relationships are based on the corruption of love and honour. And "Hamlet" is the play which Wopsle performs in, in Chapter 31.

Estella's lack of feeling creates a tension between the Romantic and the Gothic- much as Keats had done in his celebrated poem "La Belle Dame sans Merci". Dickens works hard to justify the obsessive and unrealistic approach with which Pip idolises Estella for too long as a romantic enthralment. It resembles Miss Havisham's own "unquestioning self-humiliation".

If I have a criticism of Dickens, it is that he expects us to tolerate in Pip an attitude which he expects us not to tolerate in Miss Havisham, because we know that its consequences are all bad.

Estella makes a point of stressing to Pip that, while she has a physical heart, she has "no softness there, no- sympathy- sentiment". Miss Havisham has trained these qualities out of her, and, in leaving the values of his own home and upbringing behind, in pursuing her, **Pip has misplaced his own true feeling, his ability to respond to and impart warmth.** (There is an ongoing contrast between Joe Gargery's good-heartedness and Estella's cold heartlessness). Estella stresses, again, that if she and Pip "are to be thrown much together" now, he must accept that she has no "tenderness" to bestow on anyone, and particularly on him. Pip accepts that he "should be scared" if he believes that this is true; she says that, if he chooses not to believe her, "It is said, at any rate". Even then, Pip persists in "the assurance I felt that our patroness had chosen us for one another".

When Estella looks at Pip, he is struck by a connection or association which he cannot place; he knows it is not as straightforward as picking up gestures from an adult like Miss Havisham. The repetition of the three word mantra "What *was* it?", in the form of a single paragraph, stresses that this puzzle is important. It is only solved when Pip realises who Estella's mother is, in Chapter 48 (it is Jaggers' housekeeper Molly).

Miss Havisham is "grimly playful" in this scene; she does not look at Pip, but has a "greedy look". The chandeliers are "wintry", the table is "mouldering", the room is "funereal", and Miss Havisham is "that figure of the grave", with "withered arms" and a "clenched hand".

 Although the language of death had attached to her in Chapter 8, where her dress looked "so like grave-clothes…...the long veil so like a shroud" and "she sat, corpse-like", Dickens is now describing her more, and giving her less to say. She is becoming more manic- she kisses Estella's hand "with a ravenous intensity that was of its kind quite dreadful". As fairy godmothers go, this one is starting to look like a mutation.

Then she launches into her witch-like invocation- Pip is to "Love her (Estella), love her, love her!", regardless of the pain Estella causes him. Pip, narrating, describes her intensity both as "passionate eagerness" and as "vehemence"; "it could not have sounded more like a curse". She confirms that Estella is an empty vessel, which she "adopted……bred….educated….developed" so that she may be an object of men's love. This creation of an artificial being, whose capacity to feel has been manipulated, making the monster both a victim and an agent of suffering, is redolent of

Frankenstein's monster – a comparison which Dickens uses more directly in Chapter 40.

Miss Havisham goes on to give Pip her definition of "what real love is"- "blind devotion……self-humiliation……..utter submission………giving up your whole heart and soul……..as I did!". The words are followed by "a wild cry" which expresses her inner pain.

He falls asleep that night at the Blue Boar, repeating the words "I love her" "hundreds of times" into his pillow, and disregarding the awkward question of Estella's "heart……mute and sleeping" i.e. her complete lack of feeling for him (or any other boy or man), which she has explicitly warned him of, and which Herbert raises in chapter 30.

When he arrives to pay his visit, Pip is surprised to find that Orlick has been employed as an armed doorman and security guard at Satis House. His room is "like a cage for a human dormouse", and he himself is "dark and heavy", with his loaded gun, and the understanding is that he should "give another man as good as he brought" if intruders come here. Pip will complain to Jaggers that Orlick is unfit to work at Satis House; Jaggers' dismissal of him will be another strand in the resentment which leads Orlick to try to kill Pip in Chapter 53.

Jaggers stays to dinner, and he tells Pip that Miss Havisham never eats meals, but "wanders about in the night, and then lays hands on such food as she takes"- betraying a kind of desperation and isolation which links her to the escaped Magwitch in Chapter 1. Otherwise, Jaggers behaves with "determined reticence"- because the plot demands that he says nothing which might give Pip grounds for suspicion that Miss Havisham is not his patron.

Chapter 30

After the emotionally intense preceding chapter, this one is lighter, although it contains some uncomfortable truths for Pip.

Pip mentions to Jaggers that Orlick is unsuitable as a gateman (he suspects him, because Biddy does, of the attack on Mrs Joe, and he had picked the fight in the forge with Joe in Chapter 15). He does not anticipate that Jaggers will go to dismiss Orlick immediately; Orlick will be in no doubt that Pip is responsible, and this will feed his sense of grievance even more. Pip is as perfectly <u>clear</u> about Orlick's unsuitability and untrustworthiness as he is <u>unclear</u> about Estella's.

Rather than catching the coach where Pumblechook might intercept him, Pip takes a longer walk through the town, and finds it "not disagreeable to be......recognized and stared after" as the boy who has received a fortune. But Trabb's boy ("that unlimited miscreant........his evil mind.....an invulnerable and dodging serpent") puts on an elaborate pantomime charade of fearing Pip, and then mocking his superiority.

Pip then writes to Trabb, putting in a bad word for his boy (as he had for Orlick), and perhaps intervening and using his new-found influence where he should not. He sends a gift of fish to Joe as soon as he is back in London, out of remorse and guilt for failing to visit him.

Pip cannot manage his own manservant, "The Avenger"; so he has little justification for telling other people how to treat theirs.

Pip discusses his aspirations regarding Estella with Herbert. There is a comic moment when Pip makes the dramatic confession that he loves her, only for Herbert to point out that that has always been as obvious as when Pip has had his hair cut.

Herbert, like the rest of his family, assumes that Miss Havisham is Pip's benefactor, and that she has decided, after the earlier unsuccessful trial of Estella and Herbert, to bestow her on Pip- even though Estella feels nothing for him. It is interesting that the consent of the young woman to her own marriage is still seen as optional- it would be desirable, but her adoptive parent can overrule her choice. In fact, Estella selects Drummle herself, as a man who will not be disappointed by her lack of emotional warmth, because he is just the same .

Pip asks Herbert to supply a word to describe his new status. Herbert does not use the term "gentleman", but labels Pip, more weakly, "a good fellow" with a curious mixture of attributes in his personality. Pip acknowledges that his wealth is purely due to "Fortune" (a pun), but, regarding Estella, he feels vulnerable- "dependent......uncertain.....exposed to hundreds of chances". Therefore, he says, his prospects of marrying Estella depend entirely "on the constancy of one person" – his benefactor.

Herbert remembers Pip saying that Jaggers had told Pip (in Chapter 18) that he was "not endowed with expectations only". By this, Jaggers had meant that there was money for the present, as well as the future, for Pip's living expenses and education. Matthew Pocket has told Herbert that, where Jaggers is involved, there must be a plan, which is understood to involve not *only* expectations, and therefore perhaps marriage plans, eventually; Herbert suggests to Pip, though, that if Estella has never been mentioned by name, she will not be part of it.

Challenged with this- the possibility that Estella is not intended for him- Pip has the same feeling of sadness as when he had left home at the end of Chapter 19 (the phrase "when the mists were solemnly rising" is a deliberate reference, and it recurs right at the end of the novel, in the final sentence). Then, he had felt conscious that he was leaving behind a small, safe world, and venturing into the "unknown and great"; lacking in confidence; "subdued". **Herbert is suggesting that Pip's "nature and circumstances" are so different from Estella's- because he is a Romantic and she is the opposite- that marrying her might "lead to miserable things". Pip claims that he is incapable of detaching his feelings from Estella; that it is "impossible".**

Herbert suggests that "the children of not exactly suitable marriages, are always most particularly anxious to be married", and he reveals his "secret" engagement to Clara Barley. The Pocket children all want to be married, despite the utter chaos they have grown up in with their own parents. Herbert cannot marry Clara while he has no money; the two young men are in different positions, in that **Pip has money but no fiancée and Herbert has a fiancée but no money**.

Herbert, in marrying Clara, will disappoint his own mother's expectations of a social connection- "she is rather below my mother's nonsensical family notions". His family is middle-class, hers working -class. Although such distinctions are unimportant (or false/mistaken, given the similarly obscure origins of Pip and Estella) because genuine love makes them irrelevant, Pip's pursuit of Estella is always stained with his sense of inferiority.

Pip finds in his pocket the advertisement Joe had given him for Wopsle's performance as Hamlet, and they set off to see it for themselves.

Chapter 31

Wopsle's "Hamlet" is amateurish, with a cast that is too small, unrealistic costumes, and a style of performance which, like Wopsle's own, is "very slow, very dreary". It is greeted with derision and heckling by the audience. Wopsle in particular lacks the presence or theatrical skill to make the audience believe in the drama and empathise with him.

Pip and Herbert try to leave without having to meet Wopsle, but they are accosted by "a Jewish man with an unnatural heavy smear of eyebrow"- Wopsle's dresser- who asks them to see him. Wopsle has created a pretentious title for himself- "Mr Waldengarver"- and he considers his talentless portrayal of Hamlet "a little classic and thoughtful for them here". He says that the audience- not him- "will improve" in its understanding.

Because they feel sorry for Wopsle, Pip and Herbert invite him home with them for the evening, where he regales them (not in a written out scene, but via a short narrative summary) with his vision of himself as the greatest actor of his generation.

In the previous chapter, the people in Pip's own town had been laughing at him, because of the public performance (mostly mimed) by Trabb's boy. Here, Wopsle is similarly trying to "act up" to a new role or position, and the pretentiousness of it is apparent to the public, who hoot and jeer; but he is impervious to it.

Both chapters leave the reader feeling that Pip and Wopsle lack sufficient humility (and, perhaps, modesty) to be accepted easily in their aspirations, and without fuss and some hostility and discomfort. They have both left their old worlds behind, but they expect their new worlds to recognise and accept their worth too readily, although the tone of their behaviour strikes a discordant note. Pip sympathises with Wopsle, while laughing at him "from ear to ear", because he knows himself how painful it is to be humiliated in public. His own revenge is to detach himself from Trabb as a customer, a gesture of withdrawal; Wopsle is determined that his critics will come round to his way of acting (they will not). Both approaches are ill-judged, but in some respects Pip's is even worse than Wopsle's.

The last sentence of the chapter betrays Pip's lack of self-confidence and his continuing preoccupation with Estella. He dreams that he has no money any more, and has to marry Clara (whom he has not met), or that he has to play Hamlet in front of a huge audience without knowing the lines.

Chapter 32

Estella sends Pip a typically haughty note (omitting even addressing him personally) saying that she is coming to London by coach and he must meet her. While he is waiting for her, in a state of nervous anticipation, Pip meets Wemmick, who takes him on a tour of Newgate Prison. Here are the clients whom Jaggers' defence could not save (because they were guilty). Dickens refuses to condemn them, although the legal system already has; compare the contrast Magwitch makes, in chapter 56, between a death appointed by God and a death sentence passed by a judge.

There is some **remarkably poignant and affecting writing here; the condemned "Colonel" and Wemmick have a contained conversation which alludes to his imminent execution only in euphemisms ("I shall be out of this on Monday", "if you've no further use for 'em"). Both men face his death unsentimentally, and as inevitable ("the evidence was too strong"……"Good afternoon, Colonel. Good-bye!"), even as they refuse to confront the full horror of the situation directly. Dickens slips into the narrative two details which make us empathise with the condemned man; that he had "served His Majesty" in the Army, and that he was "a very good workman" i.e. highly skilled (albeit in making false coins).** There is no other biographical detail about him, so we feel that he has been unfortunate in the course his life has taken, and that his death is an arbitrary waste of a decent man drawn into illegal behaviour. The seriousness of his position is clear from the paleness of his face, his nervous laughter and the fact that he cannot concentrate or focus- details which make us empathise with his plight.

Certainly, he is more deserving of sympathy than Orlick, who is never formally accused of assaulting Mrs Joe, because the plot requires him to be at large later on, in order to attempt to murder Pip.

Wemmick maintains his (and Jaggers') habitual professional detachment, rejecting those who cannot pay Jaggers' fees, and negotiating the gift of a pair of pigeons from the Colonel ("as far as it goes, a pair of pigeons are portable property, all the same"). Pip sees Wemmick, grotesquely, as "a gardener" inspecting his plants, and seeing which are about to die and "what other pot would go best in its place" i.e. which other prisoner awaiting trial may be able to afford Jaggers to defend him.

Wemmick meets Pip by accident, because he has been to inspect the scene of a robbery and has to speak to the accused. **For Wemmick**, it is clear, **guilt and innocence are not the important issues; all that matters is the client's ability to pay Jaggers, not the truth, or the prevailing of justice.**

Later, it will become clear that Molly may indeed be a murderer, but Jaggers has "tamed" her and saved Estella- the end justifies the means. Neither Wemmick nor Jaggers has a conscience, or a concern for truth; their behaviour is merely "professional", and **it is because he is (legally) perverting the course of justice, by securing the acquittal of the guilty, that Jaggers habitually washes his hands (like Pontius Pilate)**.

The prison guard acknowledges Jaggers' power to take "that waterside murder" and "make it manslaughter", i.e. to diminish the seriousness of a crime (as he had done with Molly, in the case which made his reputation), and Wemmick again refers to Jaggers' "immense abilities". Their time working together has taught both to **avoid awkward questions about guilt** and innocence; it is more productive, and comfortable, to concentrate on portable property, and avoid moral complications or becoming emotionally involved.

Pip still has three hours to wait for Estella's coach, and he regrets "all this taint of prison and crime". His childhood encounter with, and help for, Magwitch, and Mrs Joe's assault, his meeting with the convict's friend who gave him £2, and the reference to it in the coach by the two convicts, leaves Pip feeling that the "stain" of criminality "pervade(s) my fortune and advancement".

He feels "contaminated". Perhaps, subconsciously, he feels that he too is condemned, and that Estella is beyond his reach. His conscious feeling, again, in the last sentence of the chapter, is of "the nameless shadow"- the dream-like vision Estella reminds him of- which is, in fact, her mother, Molly.

Summary- Chapters 27-32

These chapters deal with the difficulty in adjusting to changed circumstances. Joe feels awkward with Pip, and out of place in London. Pip feels out of place in Rochester, and he will not take his manservant "the Avenger" there; Trabb's boy mocks Pip for his social pretentiousness, which is a harsh thing to do, but it emphasises that Pip can never go back to the simpler life he had as a child in Joe's house.

Shakespeare's tragedy "Hamlet" is the background to Chapter 31, and it also influences the description of the "overgrown and rank" garden at Satis House. Is it too fanciful to suggest that Dickens wants us to relate Pip's dysfunctional love for Estella to Hamlet's for Ophelia?

Dickens uses the first part of Chapter 29 to try to justify and explain Pip's obsessive and self-debasing infatuation for Estella (it is similar to Miss Havisham's former "possession" by Compeyson- note her own description of it in chapter 29). He uses Chapter 27 to present us with a parting of the ways between Pip and Joe, where Joe – a character we always sympathise with- admits his own dullness. In the light of the fact that Dickens had left his "dull" wife Kate three years earlier, and had become infatuated with Ellen Ternan, it is hard not to detect here a novelist who is using Pip as a surrogate through whom he is working out his own feelings of guilt regarding disloyalty, rejection and attraction in intimate relationships.

Orlick's appearance at Satis House, as the armed doorman, and the reappearance of the stranger who had given Pip the two pound notes (back in Chapter 10) as a convict on the coach, both serve to show how difficult it is to live a new life separate from our old one.

One of the attractions of leaving the marshes was that **Pip would escape Mrs Joe's casual violence and the criminality of local convicts; but violence (in the form of Orlick) and criminality (in the form of Magwitch and Compeyson) continue to dog him in his new life, because they are everywhere**. It is ironic that, in Chapter 32, Pip should feel such a sharp contrast between the sordid environment of Newgate Prison and Estella's beauty, because- as we will find out later- **Estella's compassion for the "wretches" in prison reflects her own close connection with the world of crime.**

Chapter 33

Dickens writes more comically here, using the waiter and the Pocket family as a source of humour. Estella is to be escorted by Pip to a house in Richmond, where she is to live "at a great expense" with "a lady….who has the power…..of showing people to me and showing me to people". She will be, as Pip realises, an object of "admiration".

Estella is typically cool, but also attentive to and mildly flirtatious with Pip; she speaks to him "slightingly, but not with displeasure", and the manner of her behaviour is "more winning" because "she cared to attract me". She says that members of the Pocket family (specifically Camilla) constantly seek to undermine his position with Miss Havisham (this reinforces the conviction that it is Miss Havisham who is Pip's benefactor), and that she takes pleasure in their failure to achieve that, just as she took pleasure in Pip's winning the fight with Herbert; she had explained, in Chapter 29, that she "took it ill that he should be brought….to pester me with his company". Here, she explains that she feels "a spirit of contempt for the fawners and plotters".

Estella has many faults, including a cruel lack of empathy, but at least she is clear and direct in what she says. Once again, she calls Pip "you silly boy" and "you ridiculous boy" when he plays the romantic with her. She makes it clear that Miss Havisham has "plans" for her, which involve constant writing, and reporting back on "how I go on- I and the jewels". **The jewels have always been released in stages, to enhance Estella's attractiveness and power over men, and she reveals that "they are nearly all mine now". The external beautifying of Estella's diamantine heartlessness, with meretricious, sparkling gems, is almost complete.**

The house where Estella is to live is "a staid old house" with ancient trees which will soon take "their own allotted places in the great procession of the dead". As Estella goes inside, and Pip watches from the outside, **we sense that this is the end of any hopes he should have that Estella is intended for him. Pip will not concede this point to himself; "still I stood looking at the house, thinking how happy I should be if I lived there with her, and knowing that I never was happy with her, but always miserable".** Our sympathy for Pip is waning because he fails to see what we can see, and what he should be seeing for himself- that Estella is controlling, wilful, cares nothing for him, and that he does not feature in Miss Havisham's plans for her.

As the narrator, Pip is clear that his hopeless, habitual search for intimacy with Estella, for "an inner meaning in her words", is futile. He thought that wherever Estella was, he could be happy, but this was self-delusion- "I was not at all happy there at the time, observe, and I knew it well". As a mature adult, writing about his young self, he is as frustrated as we are; not just with Estella, but with himself. He "went on against trust and against hope", to such an extent that he is reduced to asking a rhetorical question- "Why repeat it a thousand times? So it always was."

Towards the end of the chapter, Dickens has Pip and Estella starting a discussion about Jaggers, and Jaggers' "curious" home; but he cuts the topic off, leaving us to speculate on what connection Jaggers has with Estella. He had seemed aware of her beauty, and curiously reticent with her, in Chapter 29. We will see much later, in Chapter 51, that he has a personal interest in Estella which goes beyond the merely professional. Estella's view that those in Newgate Prison are "wretches" chimes with the authorial voice, but also reflects the fact that she is the daughter of a transported convict (Magwitch) and a murderess (Molly).

The last two paragraphs of this chapter are interesting. Matthew Pocket, they tell us, is out lecturing, and is considered an authority on the subjects of managing children and managing servants. This is very ironic, as he lives in anarchy, and has no control in his own household. Pip's delusions of his own control over his own life are similar- he sees himself as an expert on Miss Havisham's intentions, but he is not; he is only "clear and sound" about what he wishes for, even though the reality of his day to day experience contradicts his so-called expert opinion.

Chapter 34

Dickens described this novel as "a grotesque tragi-comic conception"; this chapter illustrates that very well. It opens with Pip reflecting, for perhaps the first time, on how his behaviour affects other people (badly) and, in particular, Herbert (badly). It goes on to show that Pip's irresponsible or at least casual way of life has become unsatisfying, dissolute and driven by debt. It ends with the dark news that Mrs Joe has died. This gives Pip an almost immediate further opportunity to put right the wrongs he feels he has done to Joe and Biddy, and which he reflects on in the opening paragraph.

Pip has led Herbert into debt, through his own "lavish habits", so that he is "corrupted….disturbed" "with anxieties and regrets". The worst examples of this are Pip's employment of his servant, "the canary-breasted Avenger", whom we already know of; and their application to join the unsavoury dining club "The Finches of the Grove", which the oafish Drummle (who has his own horse and cart, but cannot drive it competently) belongs to already.

Dickens goes to some trouble here to describe the psychological distress which accompanies living beyond your means- the vacillating moods ("desponding …..hopefully….drooped……deeply despondent again….we were always more or less miserable"). The most difficult part of the day is the morning, when Pip's self-loathing and self-awareness mean that he "detested the chambers beyond expression". When a letter threatening legal action over a bill for jewellery arrives, Pip shakes his servant "off his feet" in a comical outburst of misdirected anger.

Periodically, Pip and Herbert make a habit of documenting their debts, but they have nothing to pay them off with, and these sessions end, farcically, with Pip rounding the figures up with a "margin" (like an overdraft limit) which they invariably spend up to and beyond. Herbert's pride- his desire to be independent- makes it impossible for Pip to take on his debts. Herbert does not have a real job, so Pip should really be more careful not to adopt a way of life Herbert cannot afford. Pip has "grown accustomed to my expectations" and has complete "confidence in my own resources", so the sadness and hopelessness Herbert feels is much stronger than his own disingenuous way of treating debt. Pip finds that listing what they owe creates the illusion of tackling the issue, and he remains complacent, with "an admirable opinion of myself".

The overspending is really **hiding an emotional vacuum**- the "gay fiction….that we were constantly enjoying ourselves" is typical of young men ("rather common") but the underlying or "skeleton" truth is that "we never did". Lavish spending is a way of running way from this emptiness- "an infallible way of making little ease great ease". Today, we mean the same thing when we label someone a "shopaholic".

Much of this exploration of living with debt will originate in Dickens' own childhood experience, when his father went to prison for debt. But one of the central themes of the whole novel is emerging here- **money (for Pip, or Miss Havisham) does not guarantee the contentment that a modest family life does (Wemmick, Joe).**

Pip's own distress is not simply financial. He lives "in a state of chronic uneasiness respecting my behaviour to Joe" and feels guilty about how he has behaved to Biddy. He feels that his life would have been simpler if he had remained a blacksmith's apprentice, and he still feels that the forge is "home". Towards the end of the novel, under the influence of Magwitch's complete refusal to feel sorry for himself, Pip will learn that wishing your life had been different is futile, because it is the only one you have.

The black-edged letter informing Pip that Mrs Joe has died arrives, and the chapter ends with that suspenseful surprise- before Pip has had time to react to it.

Chapter 35

This chapter places the tragic and comic alongside each other; the seriousness and solemnity of Mrs Joe's funeral (which Dickens calls "the blankness of death") is subverted by the ceremonial aspects of the funeral, and by Pumblechook's silliness and insensitivity.

Trabb is the funeral director. Joe and Biddy are quiet with grief; the Hubbles are in "a decent speechless paroxysm", but walk in the procession with "excessive pride......surpassingly conceited and vainglorious"; while the "worldly-minded" Pumblechook, who is incapable of real feeling, is "alternately stuffing himself" (with plum-cake and sherry) and "making obsequious movements to catch my attention". Hubble and Pumblechook drink all of the sherry and the port, talk as though they "were notoriously immortal", and eventually go on to the Jolly Bargemen "to make an evening of it".

Once they have gone, "the house felt wholesomer"; Joe changes into more comfortable clothes, and although in Pip's presence he feels he must concentrate hard on proper table manners, he begins to relax. Biddy reminds Pip of Joe's qualities- "a strong hand, a quiet tongue, and a gentle heart"- and, in the early morning after the funeral, he is back at work "with a glow of health and strength upon his face".

Joe, with his simple and modest tastes, would have preferred a simple funeral, without Trabb's "mummery". Pip feels that the procession Trabb organises is "like a blind monster with twelve human legs, shuffling and blundering along", but they are "much admired" by the villagers, who "highly approved of these arrangements".

The noise and spectacle, and Pumblechook's bluster during the funeral service, contrast with the essential core of the event-

"*my sister was laid quietly in the earth while the larks sang high above it, and the light wind strewed it with beautiful shadows of clouds and trees*".

Joe and Biddy would welcome Pip's visits, which, Joe declares, will be "never too soon …..and never too often", but **Biddy is sceptical about whether Pip will keep his promise to visit**. Once again, he leaves Biddy on poor terms, accusing her of hurting him because she does not believe he will do what he says he will. As he leaves, Pip knows, himself, that **she is right**, and that he will not come back to the forge soon or often.

There are specific linguistic references to Pip's previous conversation with Biddy, in Chapter 19, and to Pip's hurtful criticism, then, of her for showing "a bad side of human nature", on the unjustified basis that she was "envious and grudging" of Pip's "rise in fortune". Pip's attitude to her is still condescending- we are aware that Pip is in no way better than her- but she is fiercely independent, and determined to become the local school teacher (like Jane Eyre) in order to support herself.

In the earlier chapter, Pip had criticised Joe's manners and lack of education, and Biddy had defended him, saying that Joe's natural place in society is where he is, so that Pip should not presume to take him away "into a higher sphere". Biddy had pointed out to Pip that "**a gentleman should not be unjust**", and had told him that she would "do all that lies in my power, here, at all times", to help Joe; whether or not this matches Pip's own, sentimental and disruptive idea of "improving dear Joe". Biddy helps Joe most by marrying him and giving him children, while Pip realises, too late, that Biddy would have improved him too- although she knew that Pip's obsession with Estella would always preclude him from marrying her instead.

Mrs Joe's is the first death Pip has experienced since he was very young (his brothers and his parents had died well before the opening chapter, when he was about seven). Although he does not feel "tenderness" towards her, because she had been relentless in hurting him when he was "a little helpless creature", he does feel "regret", coupled with "violent indignation" against the attacker who caused her premature death- probably Orlick.

Unfortunately (or fortunately for the plot) Orlick is stalking Biddy; he overhears Pip's assurance to her that he "would spend any money or take any pains to drive him out of that country", and this comes back to haunt Pip in Chapter 53, when Orlick has him at his mercy.

Pip reflects on his own eventual death, in the sense that he wants "others walking in the sunshine" at that time to feel sympathetic in their memory of him- "**softened** as they thought of me". **"Softened" is a word he often applies to Magwitch, as he faces his death; it is used to mean being humanised, empathetic and compassionate.**

Pip is beginning to develop some awareness of his effect on, and responsibility to, other people he cares about. But he still mismanages his relationship with Biddy, who, if he had not come into his great expectations, would have been the perfect partner for him. He is now aged around 20. His continuing condescension to her here shows that **he has still not developed truly gentlemanly qualities**. He leaves, once more, shrouded in mist- a tangible symbol of his disorientation and lack of clarity.

The seriousness of the feelings here is counterpoised by the detail with which Dickens has described the funeral. As readers, we detect Dickens' voice, as well as Pip's, in the narrative; he has drawn detailed pictures not only of the Victorian way of death, but also of the hopeless rural school, and the corruptible and impassive criminal justice system, in order to make us feel dissatisfied with the accepted way of doing these things. All three overlay an underlying emotional chaos with a controlling formality, which represses the instinct to reform and to allow true feelings to be aired and shared.

Biddy's integrity and her honest morality contrast, again, with the sentimental but irresolute promises Pip makes, to visit often. Biddy knows what is needed, to look after people and nurture them. Pip still has not found this out for himself.

Chapter 36

Pip's 21st birthday is in November, and Herbert is eight months older than him. Jaggers summons Pip to his office for a meeting at 5pm, at which he gives him £500 (a note with which Wemmick had been rubbing the side of his nose), and says that, from now on, Pip is to live on £500 p.a. until his benefactor identifies themselves; at which point Jaggers' involvement will be over.

Pip had hoped that this would be the point when he would receive some confirmation that he was to be married to Estella (because he still clings to the irrational hope that that is what Miss Havisham intends). Instead of encouragement, Pip feels "uncomfortable", and that his birthday is a non-event.

As we have found so often, Dickens writes the chapter in two parts. First, the scene in Jaggers' office is drawn comically, with Jaggers cross-examining Pip endlessly and mercilessly, particularly about the level of his spending and debt, which, he says, "I know better than you".

Jaggers' unsettling presence extends to his visit to Barnard's Inn for a meal; the effect he has on Pip is to make him "intensely melancholy" and, on Herbert, to make him feel "dejected and guilty" and of a criminal character.

The casts of the dead criminals in Jaggers' office add a touch of the macabre to the humour; they seem to be "making a stupid apoplectic attempt to attend to the conversation"; later, "the two horrible casts of the twitched faces looked….as if they….were going to sneeze".

Jaggers does volunteer one piece of information; that the timing of Pip's benefactor's self-disclosure "must not be asked" because it "might compromise" Jaggers; this is because Magwitch has already asked for Pip's address, and will, quite soon, have sailed from Australia to reveal himself.

The second scene in this chapter has Pip asking Wemmick for advice on whether he should help "a friend" (Herbert) financially. That this is Pip's instinct, as soon as he has the £500, rehabilitates him in our eyes, because we know that his own debts are at least the £700 he had computed in Chapter 34. It was in that chapter, too, that we read about Herbert's hopeless hanging around, hoping for work; and that Matthew Pocket could not or would not help Herbert to find "an opening".

Wemmick, in his professional capacity, responds to the idea of "invest(ing) portable property in a friend" "in a tone drier than any sawdust". He does not agree with Pip helping Herbert. Indeed, he tells Pip that he might as well throw his money off one of the bridges over the River Thames (because he will never see any of it again) and he conveys to Pip the sense that such an idea is a "fatal weakness". But he qualifies this by saying it is his "opinion in this office" and his "official sentiments". If he were asked at home, he might say differently, because his outlook would be affected by a different set of values and beliefs, "much as the Aged is one person, and Mr Jaggers is another".

This is a striking way of making the point that **the value of money is relative. When we view it as the means of helping a friend, of expressing affection or loyalty or responsibility, our use of it will not be** nakedly self-interested or **commercial**. There is no room for compassion or sentiment in the legal profession, but, in the parallel world of one's "private and personal capacity", our priorities, and our perception of what is worthwhile, are entirely different.

It is worth noting that £500 in Dickens' time is a very considerable or "handsome sum of money". When Miss Havisham wants to give Herbert £900 via Pip, she writes an instruction to Jaggers (in Chapter 49). Perhaps it is reasonable to suppose that the only person who has given Pip cash before (Magwitch, with the two one pound notes handed to him in chapter 10)- equally unexpected riches, in his situation at the time- is the same person who deals in ready cash here. Presumably, as a convict transported to Australia, Magwitch is unable to operate a bank account in England! Pip's powerlessness in the presence of Jaggers, too, reminds him "of that old time when I had been put upon a tombstone"; Jaggers is, by some obscure connection, here, an echo of Magwitch.

It is not straightforward to work out what the value of Pip's £500 is today. If we used the retail prices index it would be about £40,000, but on other measures of its buying power it could be many times that. The point is that it is enough money for anyone to be able to live on it without the tiniest bit of financial worry or insecurity.

Chapter 37

Pip visits Wemmick on the following Sunday, to pursue his desire to help Herbert with **a secret form of financial support (which reflects what Pip himself has benefited from)**. The Castle is an eccentric's paradise, with Wemmick's contraption which works imperfectly, and advises the Aged Parent (who is 81) when "John" is arriving, or when "Miss Skiffins" is. The Aged P is chronically deaf, but good-humoured, and Wemmick gives him tasks to do, such as making the toast and reading the paper aloud, regardless of the care someone else has to take to ensure nothing is set on fire.

Miss Skiffins, like Wemmick, is "of a wooden appearance"; her dress is "decidedly orange", her gloves "intensely green", and she is clearly "possessed of portable property". She is a "frequent visitor", Wemmick is "very regular in his walks….very regular in everything", and the domestic life here is settled, contented, and self-contained. There is an emotional intimacy between Wemmick and Miss Skiffins (he keeps trying to put his arm round her) which is completely absent between Joe and Mrs Joe. Wemmick's imagination and creativity has found an outlet in the bizarre construction of battlements and the moat and the tower and the cannon, which amounts, in the Aged P's opinion, to "this elegant and beautiful property". There is no room in Little Britain for such flights of fancy. Wemmick may be wooden there, but he is not wooden at all at Walworth. The satisfaction he, and the Aged P., derive from the years of improving the castle "by little and little" contrast with the lack of satisfaction Pip's sudden elevation has brought him.

Pip explains to Wemmick the history of his relationship with Herbert, and expresses his misgivings that **Herbert "might have done better without me and my expectations"**. Herbert's character, and his lack of resources, make Pip keen to help him, by providing "some present income-say of a hundred a year" and a capital stake which will lead to him becoming a partner in a business.

Wemmick, now that he is not at work, describes Pip's instinct to help Herbert as "devilish good", and he is persuaded to engage Miss Skiffins' brother, who is an accountant and business agent, to find Herbert a suitable business partner (the arrangements are made before the end of the chapter, but after a series of meetings with Wemmick, always away from Jaggers' office). The structure of the deal- £250 paid on inception, various payments from Pip's future income, and "some, contingent on my coming into my property"- opens the way for Miss Havisham to take over some of the financial responsibility, later, as her penance for treating Pip as a pawn in her game.

Notice how Wemmick did not come with Jaggers to Pip's rooms for his birthday meal; if Dickens had allowed him to, then the motivation for helping Herbert with money might not have been so clearly attributable to Pip, who comes to regard it as the one good deed he has done.

Summary chapters 33 -37

Both Pip and Estella are now on the verge of adulthood, and they are loosening the ties which have bound them to the older adults who have influenced and guided them (Jaggers and Miss Havisham). Estella has left Satis House for Richmond, and for a society where she will be admired and pursued by men. Pip has to take more responsibility for his own finances and debts, and he has to deal with the death of Mrs Joe. Pip and Estella will now experience greater freedom; what will they do with it?

Pip launches his plan to sponsor Herbert's career, **secretly**. This echoes the **secret kindness** of Magwitch (to him) and Joe's kindness, later, in paying Pip's debts. Jaggers hides **his secret kindness** in saving Molly and Estella, and Wemmick keeps **secret** the kindly atmosphere he has built at his home, the Castle. **The perverse normality of being afraid to be seen to be kind** is another way in which the world of "Great Expectations" is like the world of "Hamlet"- **it is only when all the secrets are exposed that life becomes healthier.**

Chapter 38

The second part of the novel approaches its conclusion with an unusually long chapter, which the end of Chapter 37 tells us will be devoted to Estella- "it is not much to give to the theme that so long filled my heart".

It is a dramatic chapter, which frames the way in which Estella now sets out to "deceive and entrap" Drummle (because of his dynastic wealth), and inserts two short dramatic scenes- in the first, which is reminiscent of Mary Shelley's "Frankenstein", Miss Havisham accuses Estella of ingratitude; and in the second, which is reminiscent of Charlotte Bronte's "Jane Eyre", Pip sees Miss Havisham wandering the corridors of Satis House, madly, after 2 o'clock in the morning, and uttering "a low cry".

Even now, Pip misinterprets Estella's role and Miss Havisham' intentions. Although Estella wonders, aloud, whether he will "ever take warning….of me", Pip persists in persuading himself that, while Estella is "set to wreak Miss Havisham's revenge on men", she will, once this instinct has been satisfied, "be given to me". When we read this, we know that Pip is mistaken, because Miss Havisham's revenge on men, through Estella, will involve righting the financial wrong which her fiancé and his collaborator had done her. She had given up her self-control, judgment and restraint, in giving in to the consuming passion she had described in chapter 29 ("real love is…blind devotion…..utter submission…..giving up your whole heart and soul"). Then, she had told Pip to love Estella because she has "bred her and educated her, to be loved"- and the instruction to love Estella is uttered with a "vehemence" which makes it seem "like a curse".

Pip is still attached to a romanticised ideal of love, and a sense that persistence and loyalty will bring the rewards they deserve ("the prize was reserved for me"). At the same time, his rational mind recognises and acknowledges that "I never had one hour's happiness in her society, and yet my mind……was harping on the happiness of having her with me unto death". It was Herbert, in Chapter 30, who had encouraged Pip to believe that "you are picked out for her and allotted to her"; Pip had responded by explaining to Herbert that his whole happiness hinged on his marrying Estella ("on the constancy of one person…….all my expectations depend").

The "great expectations" which give the novel its title are, therefore, objectively, both those (of portable "property") which Jaggers had announced

in Chapter 18, and Pip's own, very different expectations, of great happiness with Estella.

Chapter 38 is **characterised by darkness**- Pip's conversation with Estella at Mrs Brandley's house takes place "at a darkening window", at "twilight"; the candlelight at Satis House casts a "pale gloom", and the house itself is "darkened and unhealthy". In both houses, there is an emotional conflict which cannot be resolved. Estella cannot love Pip in the way he wants, and Estella cannot "love" Miss Havisham in a way which satisfies her. Miss Havisham roams the passages, moaning, "in the dark"; the dark is a metaphor both for the lack of insight which Pip and Miss Havisham exhibit, and for the imminent death, putting away or ending of relationships as they have been until now.

Miss Havisham is clearly in psychological, as well as physical, decline-"mumbling", "trembling", "witch-like", "most weird", "a mind mortally hurt and diseased", "a very spectre", "ghostly", "wasting".

But she is also "positively dreadful" in her intensity towards Estella, hanging on her "beauty….words….gestures…….as though she were devouring the beautiful creature she had reared", and clutching Estella's hand in her own.

It is amidst this grotesque and gothic scene that **Pip** is feeling his way towards the understanding which has always eluded him, while he **thought that, at Satis House, he was a character in his own fairy tale**. Now he is conscious of "the crawlings of the spiders" and "the gropings and pausings of the beetles"- of the insect life with its pointlessness, its lack of direction, and its cannibalism- and he finds himself challenging his own outlook- "I saw in everything the construction that my mind had come to, repeated and thrown back to me".

This moment of belated self-awareness is rather like the moment in a tragedy where the tragic hero realises his fatal mistake (and goes on to a clear- sighted death). There are no such consequences for Pip, because this is a tragi-comedy; he is not a tragic hero, just the hero of his own story.

Unable to sleep, Pip gets up, but sees and hears Miss Havisham's tortured wanderings, and cannot move- "I tried in the dark both to get out, and to go back, but I could do neither until some streaks of day strayed in". His inability to move is a paralysis of suspense. It is only when Estella marries Drummle, and when his benefactor reveals himself, that Pip can start to channel his emotions into productive action.

Miss Havisham's "low cry" is a wordless vocalisation of distress, which precedes a fire and/or the death of the distressed woman, who has already become a shadow or husk of a human being. The models for this are Lady Macbeth, in Shakespeare's "Macbeth" ("a mind diseased", and her guilty conscience, makes her unable to sleep), and Mr Rochester's mad first wife, Bertha Mason in "Jane Eyre". In chapter 15 of "Jane Eyre", Jane hears "a vague murmur, peculiar and lugubrious" and "a demoniac laugh", before "something gurgled and moaned" and Bertha sets the house on fire. Satis House goes up in flames in Chapter 49.

The centrepiece of this chapter is the argument between Miss Havisham and Estella. Estella points out that she is Miss Havisham's creation, and that she had not volunteered to be experimented upon- she had been a toddler at the time she was adopted- so that, if she is "cold...hard...thankless" it is because Miss Havisham has infused those qualities into her. Estella now has the upper hand in their relationship, because her "self-possessed indifference" to Miss Havisham's "wild heat" is "almost cruel", because it is "never yielding either to anger or tenderness".

In trying to manage an elderly (step)parent's fury, and accusation of a lack of love, by pointing out that she possesses and can offer "nothing" beyond "my gratitude and duty", **Estella is like Cordelia in Shakespeare's "King Lear"; she is also like Frankenstein's monster, a creature made anti-social and miserable by its creator**. Miss Havisham's "burning love" for her is like Pip's- idealistic, high-minded and unbearable. Estella uses the analogy of a child brought up to believe that daylight will harm and destroy her to explain that, if she is unemotional and unloving, it is because Miss Havisham has always told her to avoid the destructive power of loving.

The evening ends with Pip and Estella playing cards, as they had always done; "only we were skilful now, and played French games"- the innocence and childishness has gone, because they have both seen enough of the wider world to weaken Miss Havisham's controlling influence. The next morning, although everything appears to be the same as before, Pip detects that Miss Havisham is in some way afraid of Estella; that is, fearful that Estella will make her own judgments, and go her own way.

In Chapter 11, her relatives had paid Miss Havisham her birthday visit, and she had told Pip and Estella that she hoped to die on her birthday-cum-wedding day. If Miss

Havisham can no longer live out her revenge vicariously, through Estella, because Estella goes her own way, then, as Miss Havisham had put it in the earlier chapter, "the ruin is complete"; there would be nothing left for her to live for.

The final part of this chapter concerns Drummle's relationship with Estella- which Estella publicly endorses, by sending a note to the Finches' dining club- and the distress it causes Pip. Like Wopsle and Pumblechook, Drummle is a one-dimensional character who is always condemned in the same language (" the brute", "mean miserable idiot", "heavy….contemptible, clumsy, sulky…far below the average", "that hound", "the Spider", "blockhead confidence in his money", "blundering", "deficient, ill-tempered…….stupid"). Jaggers' remarks, at the end of chapter 26, that "I like the fellow….he is one of the true sort", never really ring true, because Drummle is like Orlick, but with money- but he is still nothing more than a violent, oafish thug.

Estella's intention is "to deceive and entrap" Drummle- to out-spider the spider- just as she does all men- except (or, perhaps, especially!) Pip. She sees herself as "a lighted candle", and her innumerable suitors as "moths, and all sorts of ugly creatures". The power of the lighted flame is, simply, powerful; the power of Estella's attraction is just the same- irresistible, dangerous, unfeeling, and destructive. Money, and the desire to be cruel, trump the lack of money and a desire to be kind. Joe Gargery and Herbert Pocket are weak and powerless. Miss Havisham, Estella, Magwitch, Jaggers and Drummle all belong in the monied world, because they understand the power of money and the instinct to be cruel. Pip lacks the instinct to be cruel, and so he remains a foreigner in the land of the monied and the cruel.

Chapter 39

The final chapter of the middle section of the novel brings Magwitch back into Pip's life. The weather in London is stormy and very wet (like the weather on the marshes), and Pip is "dispirited and anxious". His education with Matthew Pocket has finished; he is now 23, but unable "to settle to anything", because his understanding of his financial position is "restless and incomplete".

At 11 pm on a stormy night, Pip hears footsteps on the stairs to the top of the house where he lives (Herbert, who would be incidental here, and would get in the way of the drama, is- conveniently- abroad, so that there is a spare bedroom). Pip resents the unrecognisable stranger's warmth towards him, but then realises that it is Magwitch- "my convict". He moralises on the subject of Magwitch having "repented and recovered", but stresses (ironically) that "our ways are different ways".

Pip asks Magwitch if he has seen the man who gave him the two pounds when he was a boy; Pip insists on repaying them now, because, he says, "I have done well since". Magwitch burns the money, and asks Pip to explain his rise in the world; he hints that he knows how much money Pip has to live on, that he knows who Jaggers is; and Pip realises "the truth of my position.......its disappointments, dangers, disgraces, consequences".

Since his own expectation has always been that Miss Havisham was his benefactor, and intended Estella to be part of the "property" he would "come into", Magwitch's revelation is a ruinous emotional shock to Pip.

Magwitch has directed his obsessive desire to create (and to "own") a "London gentleman" in the same way as Miss Havisham has channelled her desire for vengeance- to give life a purpose and a focus ("This way I keep myself a going").

Pip is to Magwitch what Estella is to Miss Havisham- Magwitch thinks of himself as Pip's "second father".

But Miss Havisham's witch-like character, appearance and behaviour are all malign and destructive; Mag"witch"'s witchery is not rooted in hate, but in honour (repaying Pip's goodness to him at the start of the novel).

Magwitch's fortune has come through inheritance, from his "master", who, he says, "had been the same as me" (a shepherd? a convict?); and also from his own efforts, out of prison, where he was free to pursue his own commercial interests as " a sheep-farmer, stock-breeder, other trades besides", "it all prospered wonderful", and he "spec'lated and got rich".

Magwitch refers to himself as a "hunted dunghill dog"- an echo of his language in Chapter 3, "hunted as near death and dunghill". Pip feels "abhorrence … dread… repugnance"; he "recoiled from his touch as if he had been a snake", because he feels that Magwitch's money may be "stained with blood". Remembering that he is (allegedly) a violent criminal, Pip locks him in Herbert's bedroom for the night, partly for his own peace of mind.

Pip is speechless at first; he almost faints; he is "too stunned to think" and unable to sleep. When he eventually sleeps on the floor, he awakes at 5 a.m., in "wretchedness" and confusion. The physical surroundings reflect his mental state once more- outside, and inside, there is only "thick black darkness", because Pip's hopes of Estella are dashed, he is ashamed of the pride and social climbing with which he abandoned Joe and Biddy, and he now has the new burden of protecting Magwitch from capture and execution.

The idea that it is for Magwitch's patronage that he had left the forge leaves Pip feeling "worthless", faithless and ashamed; he had "deserted Joe", not for a place in respectable society (with Estella) from which he could help Joe up, but for an obligation to an escaped and condemned convict whose fortune is anything but respectable.

The second of the three volumes ends, therefore, with Pip just as miserable as he was as a small child. He has money, where he had none; he has a "second father", where he had none.

But, where he dreamed of an intimate relationship with Estella, he has an intimate connection with Magwitch, for whom he will now have to take on the permanent (parental) responsibility of keeping him safe from arrest.

In the absence of the facts, Pip had constructed his own reality, in which Miss Havisham was his patron and Estella his future wife. While not knowing the true source of his "great expectations" has been unsettling, knowing the truth now is, arguably, worse, because in an instant it has stripped away his romantic hopes, and replaced dreams with dangers.

Whether or not Pip is worse off than before, emotionally, if not financially, is a hypothetical question, because there is no going back- "I could never, never, never, undo what I had done". This repetition of "never" recalls the final speech of King Lear in Shakespeare's play- "Thou'lt come no more,/Never, never, never, never, never!"- where he mourns the death of his child. Pip, too, recognises that, for him, **this is the end of his childhood**. He feels that he has failed in his responsibility to Joe and Biddy. Now he must not fail in his enforced and reluctant responsibility to Magwitch.

Summary - Chapters 38-39

Sometimes it is better not to know what you have been waiting to find out; with the revelation that his benefactor is Magwitch, not Miss Havisham, Pip's hopes regarding Estella become futile, and his dreams must be replaced by a harsher reality.

Miss Havisham has accused Estella of ingratitude (a recurring theme in the novel), and Estella has pointed out that she is what Miss Havisham has made her into. Miss Havisham is less a benefactor or mother to Estella than a predator who is set to "devour" her. Miss Havisham, like Magwitch, has a central focus- to settle a score with society through her control of a young adult- which is doomed to fail, because Estella sees, feels and rejects the emptiness of being a bauble, just as Pip rejects the financial trappings of being a gentleman, because they, too, are empty and unsatisfying.

One of the benefits of Dickens' three volume structure is that they separate Pip's childhood, adolescence and adulthood into distinct stories within the novel. They perform the same function for Estella, too.

Cast List and Chapter Locations- Book Two

As with Book One, use this handy checklist to save time and speed your revision. In particular, if you want to spend a session studying one particular character, use this list to find when – and the location where - they appear.

Chapter 20 Pip at Jaggers' office and in the adjacent streets; with Jaggers

Chapter 21 Pip and Wemmick walk to Barnard's Inn; Pip meets Herbert Pocket there

Chapter 22 Pip and Herbert at Herbert's home; Pip arrives at Matthew Pocket's

Chapter 23 Pip and the Pocket family, their servants and their house-guests (Drummle and Startop) at their house

Chapter 24 Pip, Wemmick, Jaggers at Jaggers' office; Jaggers in court

Chapter 25 Wemmick entertains Pip at home; with the "aged parent"

Chapter 26 Jaggers entertains Pip, Herbert, Startop and Drummle at his home; with Molly the housekeeper

Chapter 27 Pip and Joe at Barnard's Inn; with Herbert

Chapter 28 Pip's journey back to Rochester by coach; with the two convicts; and at the Blue Boar

Chapter 29 Pip at Satis House- meets Orlick, Miss Havisham and Estella, Jaggers, Sarah Pocket

Chapter 30 Pip provokes Jaggers into sacking Orlick; Trabb's boy mocks Pip in the street; back at home, Pip and Herbert

Chapter 31 Pip, Herbert, Wopsle (and his dresser) at the theatre and at Barnard's Inn

Chapter 32 Pip and Wemmick at the coach office and in Newgate jail; they meet the condemned "Colonel"

Chapter 33 Pip and Estella at the coaching inn and to Richmond, Surrey, and to the house where she is to stay

Chapter 34 Pip and Herbert at home

Chapter 35 Pip, Joe and Biddy at the forge, and at Mrs Joe's funeral (with Pumblechook and the Hubbles); Orlick, unseen

Chapter 36 Pip's 21st birthday; at Jaggers' office, with Jaggers and Wemmick, and at Barnard's Inn, with Herbert and Jaggers

Chapter 37 Pip and Wemmick, at Wemmick's home, the Castle, with the Aged Parent and Miss Skiffins

Chapter 38 Pip and Estella at Richmond and at Satis House, with Miss Havisham; Pip at the Finches; Pip and Estella at a ball at Richmond

Chapter 39 Pip and Magwitch at Pip's house, Garden-Court, in the Temple, by the River Thames

Chapter 40

Magwitch's arrival changes the focus of the novel and the nature of its suspense. From wondering who Pip's benefactor is, we now wonder whether Pip can keep Magwitch safe. Magwitch is essentially a new, major character, and Dickens takes the opportunity to bring him to life.

There is plenty of humour here, in the uncouthness of Magwitch's habits, and in Pip's very real misgiving that, in every small action of Magwitch's, "there was Prisoner, Felon, Bondsman, plain as plain could be". Pip's very natural and believable fear that Magwitch will be identified contrasts with Magwitch's own attitude, which is brave, realistic, and pragmatic; a man who has spent most of his life in adverse circumstances is not inclined to stop taking reasonable risks, or fail to enjoy the freedom he has waited for for so long. What the law-abiding and inexperienced Pip sees as rash, the hardened criminal sees as normal.

As readers, we are not so confident, because of the mysterious and unidentified man Pip trips over on the stairs- a man who may well be following Magwitch, and who, we find out later (in Chapter 53) is Orlick.

As Magwitch comes into the heart of the plot, so Jaggers will recede; Pip is an adult, has free access to the money, and Magwitch's "long account" with Jaggers (whom he had saved at his trial for a crime, the details of which he will not disclose) is settled.

Pip visits Jaggers to ask whether Miss Havisham has not, after all, been involved in his "expectations"; Jaggers confirms that it is only Magwitch, and that **Pip should have concentrated on "the evidence"**. Comically, Jaggers and Pip pretend to each other that Magwitch is still is Australia, while they both know he is nearby, and has made himself known through "verbal communication". Jaggers tells Pip that he had warned Magwitch that, if he came back to England, he would make himself "liable to the extreme penalty of the law".

In fact, the death penalty for the crime of returning from transportation to Australia had last been imposed in 1810, although it remained technically in force until 1835. The jeopardy which Magwitch faces - life or death- is much more effective than a potential jail term, and makes for a more compelling plot, which is why Dickens takes a liberty with historical accuracy here.

Just as Pip has to adjust his romantic temperament, in order to become more pragmatic, Magwitch arrives; and Magwitch is the arch-pragmatist. Where Pip imagines spies and informants on every corner, and self-disclosure in every mannerism of Magwitch, Magwitch himself, having said that "caution is necessary", points out that disguises are effective; that he is not well known in London; that he has no intention of announcing his arrival in the newspapers. Instead, like an old bird which has escaped many snares, he will perch on a scarecrow, and "if there's Death hid inside of it, there is, and let him come out, and I'll face him, and then I'll believe in him and not afore".

Magwitch is a figure of integrity, and he keeps this promise, just as he has kept his promise to himself about repaying his debt to Pip. **He faces his own death with conspicuous courage**, and he is depicted, throughout the novel, as a decent and honourable man, who has fallen foul of the law for no other reason than he was born to be a "warmint". Just as when we toured Newgate Jail with Wemmick in Chapter 32, Dickens wants us to empathise with those who find themselves condemned, rather than judging them.

This would be harder to achieve if we were given details of Magwitch's crimes; and it is easier to achieve when the "Colonel" is a forger, not a killer. Justice and truth, as Wemmick and Jaggers prove, through their use of the witness-buyer Mike, are malleable, and capable of being manipulated. So some are victims of it (whether they have committed the crime or not they get punished), while others- Orlick- go free and remain a threat to society.

Being "professional" in Little Britain is a matter of money and results; but **the emotional centre of the novel is not in Little Britain- it is in Walworth with Wemmick, and on the marshes, where the novel started, with Joe, Biddy, Pip and Magwitch.**

Suffering, making mistakes and learning from them, humanises us; commercial success or inherited money (Jaggers, Pumblechook, Miss Havisham and Estella, Mrs Brandley) do not.

Magwitch's ungainly habits add to the sense of his character. He has a strange card game, he mops up everything on his plate because he has lived so long in prison, then there is his smoking, his odd dress sense, his insistence on swearing on the Bible. This is strengthened by his unattractive appearance and his dog-like eating habits (he apologises to Pip for being "a heavy grubber"). But none of these off-putting characteristics can undermine his essential humanity and nobility, or his courage in adversity. He refuses to be "low", or to feel sorry for himself; he is content with whatever comes his way; he is altruistic, and wants only good things for Pip, but without the destructive emotional control Miss Havisham seeks over Estella. A character who seeks social mobility, not for himself, but for someone else, has a sound basis for engaging a reader's sympathy and support.

The "lurker on the stairs", and the danger Magwitch is in, make Pip "prone to distrust and fear". They also make it impossible for him to explore his own feelings about Magwitch and Estella as he would otherwise have been able to do. He does, though, feel "chained to" his benefactor, and despairs that Magwitch has no intention of leaving the country. The more Pip recoils from Magwitch, "the more he admired (Pip) and the fonder he was". It is as though Magwitch has been visited on Pip, to see whether he can look after someone, in the way he has failed to look after Joe, Mrs Joe, or Biddy. It is like a test, that we, the reader, get to mark, and the question is: **does he, after all, have the instincts of a gentleman, or not?**

Chapter 41

Dickens uses a conversation between Pip and Herbert (just back from France) to explore what is to be done about Magwitch/Provis. Pip is determined not to be in his debt, and so to renounce his patronage and seek to pay back the money he has had. Herbert points out that having risked so much to return and see Pip, Magwitch might, if confronted with this intention, deliberately surrender himself, to be executed, in despair- in which case Pip would have to live with the guilt of having been responsible for his death.

While Magwitch is in England, he could use the threat of handing himself in to force Pip (and Herbert) to spend his money in all kinds of flashy ways. The best option, therefore, is to take him abroad, somewhere- anywhere!- where the death penalty will not apply; then Pip can "extricate" himself by cutting his financial ties with Magwitch. Doing that will put Herbert's career and marriage plans in jeopardy (because Pip is paying for them out of Magwitch's money), but Pip cannot reveal that complication, or deal with it, at this stage.

The next morning, they ask Magwitch to tell them about his struggle with the other convict on the marshes; partly to judge how capable of violence he is, in general; and partly in order to find out more about his story (which will enable Dickens to add depth to his character, and paves the way for the hidden connection to be revealed between Magwitch and the two men who duped Miss Havisham, as related to Pip by Herbert in Chapter 22).

Chapter 42

Magwitch explains part of his life story; he is a habitual, career criminal out of necessity. His lack of education defines him, and has consigned him to the society of an underclass - criminals, a deserting soldier and an itinerant, freakish giant. Magwitch explains eloquently how he "got to be a man"- through a series of occupations "that don't pay and lead to trouble". He expresses no self-pity at all.

One of the things which links him and Pip is the harshness of their childhoods; Pip has acquired a little education, and had the Gargerys to look after him, and a roof over his head. Magwitch was treated, as a child, as a "hardened" felon, a moral outcast. At the Christmas meal in Chapter 4, the adults had sermonised on Pip's degradation, and Magwitch was subjected to the same treatment, being given moralistic tracts and sermons, and having his head measured by phrenologists to see whether he had the physiology of a subhuman criminal.

The narrative, which, for once, is not really Pip's, but Magwitch's, depicts three scenes vividly. These are: Compeyson's grooming and professional seduction of Magwitch (merely by providing him with food); the death of Compeyson's previous henchman, whose "surname" was Arthur (Magwitch is wrong in recalling this detail- it was his first name); and his joint trial with Compeyson.

Compeyson has haunted the novel, although he has made only the briefest of appearances in it so far. He is a smooth but sinister and exploitative figure, who takes advantage of other people's misfortunes and exposes them to the dangers which he will not accept himself. It is because of his ease with "the ways of gentlefolks", his good looks and careful elegance ("he has a watch and a chain and a ring and a breast-pin and a handsome suit of clothes") that Compeyson is plausible, and able to operate in "swindling, handwriting, forging, stolen bank-note passing" and other criminal frauds. He is addicted to gambling.

Compeyson and Arthur "had been in a bad thing with a rich lady some years before, and they'd made a pot of money by it". Herbert realises, and tells Pip, that this was Miss Havisham, and that Compeyson was her truant fiancé. Magwitch describes him as "as cold as death": This is a direct echo of where, in Chapter 8, Pip describes Miss Havisham, at his first visit, as sitting "corpse-like."

The death of Arthur is dealt with in a memorable way; Arthur (whom Herbert recognises, not as a man whose surname is Arthur, but as Miss Havisham's half-brother), is suffering from "the horrors" and sees a ghost (the ghost of Miss Havisham, seeking its revenge on him) which is bearing a shroud to wrap him in. His death, at the time of Magwitch's arrival, creates the opening for Magwitch to become Compeyson's assistant.

When they are tried, the jury cannot see beyond the surface- Magwitch's lack of eloquence and social connections, his scruffiness and his criminal record earn him a fourteen-year prison sentence. Compeyson's sentence, by unjust contrast is seven, because of his apparently "good character and bad company". The verdict is especially unjust, because the good character belongs to Magwitch and the bad company is Compeyson; but Compeyson can manipulate "justice" because he is smarter than Magwitch (just as Jaggers is smart, and manipulates juries).

Magwitch had found himself compelled to help Compeyson, and join him in his criminality, just as Pip had found himself compelled to be an accessory to Magwitch in taking the pork pie and the brandy and Joe's file.

Compeyson takes on more reality, as Magwitch speaks of him more. Where Magwitch held Pip upside down and scared him just enough to guarantee his co-operation in Magwitch's time of need, Compeyson is colder, calculating and extremely manipulative. We will see how he has manipulated Orlick too, to secure his loyalty.

We now understand that **Magwitch's apparent tendency to be violent is not pathological, but is directed only at Compeyson, because of the way he had exploited him**, and the consequences of that. He had promised Compeyson that he would "smash that face of his", and, having attacked him on the prison ship, and in the marshes, Magwitch was transported to Australia as a punishment for "my murderous intentions". It is ironic that Magwitch understands the true nature of crime and justice for criminals; the legal system of their day, as shown in this book, does not. Magwitch alone understands how, to be just, the punishment should fit the crime.

The chapter ends with Herbert making the link between Compeyson and Arthur and Miss Havisham. Magwitch has hinted at his misfortunes in marriage ("My Missis as I had the hard time wi' ") before stopping himself; **the narrative would be spoilt if Dickens went on at this point to explore Magwitch's parenthood (of Estella), which is to be the final surprise in the novel, and the last piece of the jigsaw which links the characters' lives together.**

Summary- chapters 40-42

Magwitch bursts on to the stage of the novel, as he did at the very start; Pip's uninvited guest. Until he discovers the identity of his benefactor, Pip is miserable, directionless; but when he finds it is Magwitch, he is plunged into the horrors of a ghost-story, a gothic nightmare of running away and pursuit. Pip reflects, ruefully, that "a ghost could not have been taken and hanged on my account". Magwitch is not so much a ghost as a dead man walking. Jaggers is very clear with Pip about the fact that Magwitch, if caught, will be executed. Pip can barely sleep, and he is in a state of continual anxiety.

Magwitch's generosity is boundless- he regards everything he has as belonging to Pip, "my London gentleman" and "the gentleman what I made". Pip resolves not to take any more of Magwitch's money, and Herbert formulates a plan- Pip must take Magwitch abroad and then detach himself from Magwitch. The idea that Magwitch might give himself up (to be hanged) if Pip denies him his wish-fulfilment so soon is convincing, and it sustains the plot.

The story of Magwitch's deprived childhood and pitiful life is graphically alive. Note how Compeyson's advantages- good looks, good education, good manners- made his prison sentence lighter and Magwitch's even harsher. Note, too, that, in the wonderfully gothic description of the death of Arthur Havisham, it is a ghostly version of Miss Havisham who comes with a shroud to take him to death, because he had swindled her.

The connection between Magwitch, Compeyson and Miss Havisham is clear to Herbert and Pip. The burden Pip now bears- of keeping Magwitch undetected- is even heavier because Compeyson fears him so much, and will certainly betray him if he finds him (as the arch-villain surely will). He feels like the student Frankenstein, who created a monster (Magwitch is Pip's monster) who dogs him. He also has to absorb the disappointment that Miss Havisham is not his patron, and Estella not intended for him. Jaggers (who had defended Magwitch in court, without success) is as dispassionate as ever. He tells Pip that, instead of making assumptions about Miss Havisham, he should have examined the "evidence". This is ironic, because Jaggers is the arch-manipulator of evidence.

Although Dickens makes Pip's servants the subject of some humour, these chapters are dark; haunted by ghosts, monsters and the prospect of Magwitch's death, if betrayed. The darkest note comes with the "lurker on the stairs", whom Pip trips over. There is a tiny, hidden clue to who he is- the gateman tells Pip that he wore "dust-coloured" clothes and a dark coat. When Pip sees a man who reminds him of Orlick, in Chapter 43, that man is also "dust-coloured".

Pip abhors Magwitch for his ugliness, his uncouth manners and his crimes, the details of which Magwitch refuses to disclose. Readers, though, see that Pip, as a child, barely escaped such a life; he was called "swine" and "naturally wicious", just as Magwitch was labelled a hardened criminal from a tender age. Compeyson's education has saved him, so that he can commit more wrongs; and Pip's (very basic) education by Biddy, and his being given a home by Joe and Mrs Joe, saved him from having to steal turnips, as the orphan Magwitch had been forced to do. Now Pip lives in the shadow of Newgate prison, and his revulsion for all things criminal until now is about to be transformed into compassion for the downtrodden criminalised class.

Chapter 43

Pip feels especially keenly the contrast between his own criminal connections (Magwitch) and Estella's "pride and beauty", which he thinks belongs to a completely different world. Ironically, he will discover that while his link with Magwitch is only a financial connection, Estella's is that of child-parent, so that Estella is connected to the criminal underworld, too. Magwitch regards himself as Pip's "second father".

The suspense over the delay in leading up to the revelation of Estella's parentage has been managed very carefully; firstly by means of the vague connection Pip made between Estella's mannerisms and hand movements, and Molly's; secondly, by Magwitch's omission of discussing his marriage- he just alludes to it in Chapter 42- and his omission to press Pip, in Chapter 39, on the identity of Pip's romantic object ("Isn't there bright eyes somewhere, wot you love the thoughts on?").

Magwitch has told Pip and Herbert that he does not know whether Compeyson is still alive (or at large). Pip is aware, as Magwitch seems not to be, that Compeyson would have every reason to find Magwitch and betray him to the police.

Having resolved not to take any more money from Magwitch, Pip decides that, before he arranges to take him abroad, to relative safety, he must go to see Estella and Miss Havisham. Estella has already left Mrs Brandley's, for Satis House, without Pip taking her- an odd departure from the previous routine, which, we soon find out, is because she is now escorted by Drummle, whom she is about to marry.

Pip pretends to Magwitch that he is going to see Joe, and when he arrives at the Blue Boar for breakfast Drummle is there.

Their last encounter was a confrontation over Drummle's social connection with Estella, which Pip had challenged and found incredible. Now Dickens uses a comic approach to dramatise the tension between them- by making them jostle over possession of the fireplace (shoulder to shoulder and toe to toe). The fireplace is a surrogate for Estella.

Drummle hints at the awful truth when he advises Pip not to lose his temper, and asks him, with uncharacteristic insight, "Haven't you lost enough without that?". Pip knows that Drummle is there to continue his romantic pursuit of Estella ("the lady")- even that is "poisonous" to Pip; his "insolent triumph" exasperates Pip, and engenders in him "a tingling in my blood" and "smouldering ferocity", and it offends us too, because Drummle has nothing to be so self-satisfied about, with his "blundering brutal manner".

These feelings of Pip's, as he finally realises that he has no chance of winning the girl he has set his heart on, echo, in some sense, the feelings with which Orlick resents Pip as someone who has thwarted his prospects with Biddy (both of them having little regard for the girl's feelings on the subject of a potential relationship with them). Once again, the line between the trappings of a gentleman and the psychology of a violent and hateful criminal mind is very fine.

When Drummle demands a light for his cigar, after mounting his horse, Pip thinks that the man who provides it "reminded me of Orlick". This, like the unidentified man ("a lurker") on the stairs in Chapter 40, seems of no significance, but it becomes significant in hindsight, when Orlick reveals the extent of his grudge against Pip (in Chapter 53), and his connection with Compeyson. **Dickens is using the limited vision of Pip as the narrator to sustain and build mystery and tension in the narrative**; Pip is overlooking details, and we understand why- he is preoccupied with the danger to Magwitch, and his disappointment that Estella cannot be for him.

Two things are happening here, which make us more sympathetic towards Pip than we have been before. He is bearing his sufferings with dignity (rather like Magwitch), and he is finally confronting the end of the fantasy world of the fairy tale in which he had indulged, despite what Jaggers calls the "evidence". The mature way in which Pip faces his powerlessness makes us feel that we are strongly on his side.

Chapter 44

Pip arrives at Satis House to find Miss Havisham (watching) and Estella (knitting) - he announces that he is "as unhappy" as Miss Havisham could ever have wished, because he has now found out who his true patron is ("not a fortunate discovery"). He wishes he had never left his village; he realises, now, that he was merely a minor pseudo-employee of Miss Havisham's, "a kind of servant, to gratify a want or a whim, and….be paid for it".

She becomes angry when he suggests that it was not "kind" to let him continue to misunderstand her intentions towards him, and to reinforce the misunderstanding by encouraging her relatives to suspect that she was preferring Pip financially to them. Miss Havisham's defence is that "you made your own snares. I never made them."

Pip commends Matthew and Herbert Pocket to her, because they were friendly to him after they thought he had "superseded them". He labours the point that they are "incapable of anything designing or mean" and that, in comparison with her other relatives, "they may be of the same blood, but…..they are not of the same nature".

It is an interesting distinction. In Chapter 4, Mr Hubble had said that Pip was "naterally wicious"- though the viciousness was all in Pip's sister, Mrs Joe. **Some characters are undoubtedly vicious- above all, Compeyson, but also Miss Havisham, Orlick, Pumblechook, Drummle, Bob Barley, Camilla, Mrs Joe and Molly, and- according to Pip- Trabb's boy. Magwitch, and various other condemned criminals, may appear vicious, but any vicious behaviour on their part has been provoked, and is excusable (Miss Havisham's thirst for revenge is not). Estella has been made vicious, by her adoptive mother, and she has to marry Drummle to realise that this is no way to live.**

Joe, Biddy, Clara, Herbert and Matthew Pocket and Wemmick are not vicious. Jaggers is probably not naturally vicious, but he can be when "professional".

Pip is not vicious, although he has been "brought up by hand" to believe that he is; he has been "mean" and condescending to Joe and Biddy. He and Biddy, though, are essentially "of the same nature", and, but for the great expectations which took Pip away from the forge, he would have married her, and there would have been no novel.

Both Pip and Estella have to adjust their expectations – of themselves and other people- before their happiness as adults can become possible; a quest which lies at the heart of many 19th-century novels, from Jane Austen onwards.

Pip asks Miss Havisham to take on the financial obligation he has for Herbert's career development (because, without money from Magwitch, he will be unable to meet the commitments he had made), but he asks for nothing for himself (just as Joe had).

Pip declares his love for Estella, who is very slow to respond in words. Instead, **there is a strong focus here on her hands**, while she knits- "the action of her fingers…..in the action of Estella's fingers…..her fingers plied their work….with her fingers still going…perfectly unmoved and with her fingers busy". She continues to knit because she is immune to feeling; so, when Pip announces that he loves her, she hears "sentiments, fancies…….which I am not able to comprehend". Only after this does she set aside the knitting- "Her fingers stopped for the first time, as she retorted rather angrily".

Hands- Jaggers' and Molly's- had been equally dominant in Chapter 26- the only time Molly has appeared so far. The concentration on hands and fingers in that chapter is intended as a subliminal suggestion of the true relationship between Molly and Estella.

Pip argues that such deadness of feeling surely "is not in Nature"; she points out that "it is in the nature formed within me". Similarly, he had accused Biddy (in Chapter 19) of having "a bad side of human nature", when she did not see Joe's happiness in the same, "improved" form he envisaged for Joe. And the incapacity to love, or receive love, explains and motivates Estella's decision, which she reveals to Pip now, that she will marry Drummle very soon. Her argument is that to marry someone who does love her would be cruel to them; that, in marrying Drummle, there will be no disappointment on either side; and that she is marrying now out of boredom- "I am tired of the life I have led, which has very few charms for me, and I am willing enough to change it".

Pip's "bitter tears" fall fast on Estella's hand; and he "held her hand to my lips some lingering moments" after he has said all he has to say.

Miss Havisham watches this discussion of the meaning and nature of love with "her hand to her heart". Pip's despair at the news that Estella is to marry Drummle brings from Miss Havisham "a ghastly look" and then "a ghastly stare of pity and remorse"; she realises what a monster she has created, and that the form her revenge on men has taken has gone too far, because Pip is an innocent victim, and not a boy who deserved to have his feelings punished like this.

Pip is so distressed that he cannot face the coach trip back to London, or the possibility of seeing Drummle at the inn, so he walks the 26 miles home. **The chapter ends with another dramatic twist; Wemmick has left him a note warning him, simply, "Don't go home".**

Chapter 45

This chapter is in two parts. First, in comic/gothic mode, Pip stays in a creepy hotel; secondly, he goes to Wemmick's to find out what he meant in his note.

Anyone who has received such a note will expect to have a sleepless, "miserable" and "uneasy" night; Dickens exaggerates the effect by having Pip remember that a man had killed himself at that hotel, so that he imagines that must have happened in the room he is in.

He walks to Wemmick's house, so that Wemmick can tell him in private what he could not say in the office- that **Magwitch's absence from Australia is well known in the prison community, leading to speculation that he may have returned to England; and that Pip's home has been watched, and may still be being watched, by someone who has an interest in locating Magwitch.**

Just as with Pip's conversation with Jaggers about Magwitch's return to London, here, Wemmick passes information by nodding, as though (with no-one else present apart from the profoundly deaf Aged P.) speaking could incriminate him. Behind the comic charade is the ominous fact that **Compeyson is in London.** Wemmick advises Pip to keep Magwitch hidden in London ("Don't break cover too soon"); he and Herbert have already moved Magwitch to lodge with Clara Barley at Mrs Whimple's. Wemmick knows how criminals think, and so he is adept at laying false trails, because, as he says to Pip, "you want confusion".

The light-heartedness, which includes Pip setting fire to the Aged P's breakfast sausage, and the emphasis that the meat is from the pig at Wemmick's self-sufficient smallholding ("Do try him, if it is only for old acquaintance sake"), does not hide the underlying seriousness. We now know that Compeyson is looking for Magwitch; and we know what a threat that is, because of the manufactured death penalty Dickens has jeopardised Magwitch with.

Wemmick warns Pip to "avail yourself of this evening to lay hold of his portable property.....don't let anything happen to the portable property". It is advice Pip does not take, because of his aversion to taking advantage of what he sees as the proceeds of crime- a principled position which will, later, leave him even poorer than he needs to be.

Summary- chapters 43-45

Pip has to face the fact that his hopes or expectations of Estella will not be fulfilled, not just because Miss Havisham is not his benefactor, but also because his association with the tainted character of Magwitch makes him feel less worthy of her. This turns out to be supremely ironic once we know- later- that Magwitch is Estella's father.

Pip's meeting with Drummle, with its petty territorial and face-saving rituals, is bitter-sweet. The comedy does not mask Drummle's thuggish ability to win (Estella has chosen him precisely for his lack of feeling). Just as Herbert fought Pip naively in the garden of Satis House, Pip has fought Drummle naively for Estella- and lost. We share the feelings of powerlessness and frustration which Pip experiences, but does not articulate in the narrative.

When Pip tells Miss Havisham how unhappy he is, she says that being kind, or alerting people to "snares", is not her responsibility. Pip speaks of what is honest/false/base/wrong; of "nature"; and of his love for Estella, who, at this key moment, is "unmoved". It is she, not Magwitch, who is the monster; and it is Miss Havisham, not Pip, who is the scientist who created the monster which Estella has become. Estella reminds Pip, dispassionately, of what she had told him - of her incapacity to feel love or respond to being loved. It is because of this disability that Drummle is a suitable husband for her; a man whom she has chosen for herself, and whom Pip- whom she calls "you visionary boy"- calls a "stupid brute". This is enough to awaken "pity and remorse" in Miss Havisham, though not in Estella.

Wemmick's warning that Pip should not "go home" commits Pip to a night in the haunted Hummums hotel. Wemmick confirms to Pip that he is being watched, and that Compeyson is alive, and in London; that hiding Magwitch with Clara is a good idea; and that Pip should secure Magwitch's portable property for his own use (which Pip has no intention of doing).

In these chapters, we see Pip starting to make, and to assert, moral judgments. Where Miss Havisham, Estella and Wemmick are wrong, he is not afraid to take a different view, and to take his own path.

Chapter 46

Pip goes to see Magwitch at his new lodgings, where Clara's gout-ridden, ogre-like, bedridden father is heard but never seen; he meets Clara for the first time. She has refused to meet him earlier in his friendship with Herbert, because she thought Pip was extravagant and frivolous.

Unlike the dysfunctional relationship between Pip and Estella, overseen by Miss Havisham, the "motherly" Mrs Whimple has "fostered and regulated" Herbert's engagement to Clara "with equal kindness and discretion".

Old Barley is noisy and "truculent"; he doles out his and his daughter's food as though he were still on a ship and in charge of its supplies (another comical counterpoint to Miss Havisham's inability to live in the present, and her attachment to the past, which she is determined to perpetuate daily).

Pip finds Clara immensely charming, and regards her "with pleasure and admiration". Amusingly, he says that he would not have wished her and Herbert apart not for a large sum of money, but, instead, "for all the money in the pocket-book I had never opened". This is the "portable property" which Magwitch has told Pip is considerable, and which Pip should take and use.

Another touch of humour comes in the narrative technique; Pip (as narrator) repeats, in writing, the sea-shanty Bill Barley sings about himself, but with the substitution of positive language for the swear words in the original ("I substitute good wishes for something quite the reverse").

When the writing lapses into a more serious style, it is to tell us that Magwitch, here, **"was softened"- "indefinably……..but certainly"** (refer back to the analysis of Chapter 35, and you will see how Dickens uses the term "softened" as a stage in our preparing for death). Here it means too that he is reconciled to anything which may happen. He is not frightened, or concerned, at having been moved. He is "very reasonable" and less insistent on the idea that he wants to see Pip spending his money like a gentleman. He appreciates that coming back was dangerous, or "a venture", but he has no intention of turning it into "a desperate venture". **Pip omits to tell him that Compeyson is looking for him**, so Magwitch still believes that, with Pip, Jaggers, Wemmick and Herbert all caring about his situation, "he had very little fear of his safety with such good help".

We have already seen that, in the world of this novel, **keeping secrets complicates lives**. Pip protects and preserves Magwitch's sense of contentment by giving him no indication of the danger he is in (from Compeyson), and by concealing from him the fact that when he is recaptured all his wealth and property is confiscated, so that his dream for Pip is destroyed. The other great secret which Pip has not revealed at the end of the novel is that Estella is Magwitch's daughter- see the analysis of Chapter 51 for more on this. Matthew Pocket is a gentleman partly because he was brave enough to confront Miss Havisham with the unpleasant truth about her fiancé. Pip seems to be learning that **the moral responsibility of a gentleman may extend sometimes to protecting others from the unbearable impact of the truth.**

As Pip leaves, with the intention of staying away from the riverside house, in case he is being followed, he goes down the staircase and reflects on the night of Magwitch's arrival up the stairs at his home- then, he had "little supposed my heart could ever be as heavy and anxious at parting from him as it was now". Perhaps, psychologically, **the care and attention he wanted to give Estella is being directed to Magwitch instead; appropriately enough, in the light of their yet to be revealed relationship.** Magwitch has now dropped his seaborne alias of Provis, and is to be known as "Mr Campbell".

Pip reflects on the affectionate and caring atmosphere at Mrs Whimple's; he senses it as "overflowing" with "redeeming youth and trust and hope". This is an ironic contrast with Satis House- "Satis" meaning, originally, that those who lived there had everything they could need or want; but **Satis House is now a place which Pip, and we, have had enough of, in its negative energy** and emotion, and its perverse sense of how people should behave to each other.

Pip hires a rowing boat, and he practises rowing it down the river (with and without Herbert) as a preparation for Magwitch's escape. He cannot rid himself of the suspicion that he is being watched. While Herbert sees the river as a metaphor of good things coming towards Clara and him, Pip, who is "dispirited", fears that the river flows towards Magwitch bearing "his pursuers, going swiftly, silently, and surely, to take him". Again, a chapter which has strained to be light and positive ends in a minor key.

Chapter 47

What the plot needs now is some proof that Wemmick is right, and that the prison gossip is true; **that Compeyson is close to discovering Pip or Magwitch or both.** If the plot is to move towards a final, dramatic confrontation, the threat of **Compeyson needs to come out of the shadows and more firmly on to the stage of the novel. Dickens does that in this chapter.**

Again, the threat and danger is juxtaposed with a grotesque, comic scene. Pip has nothing to do, so he goes to the theatre to see Wopsle's latest performance. Wopsle, too, has seen his great expectations of London go unfulfilled. He had had grandiose ideas about his skill as a great tragic actor, but his performance in "Hamlet" was laughable. Now, he is still in the theatre, but the parts he is playing are unglamorous, and the plays are pantomimes, not serious dramas.

Pip has to sell jewellery in order to settle debts, because he regards using any more of Magwitch's money as "a heartless fraud". He has sent the "unopened pocket-book"- the "portable property", which Wemmick told him to secure – back to Magwitch, via Herbert.

Pip has a nagging sense that by now Estella has married Drummle, but he avoids anything which might confirm that fear. Pip the narrator asks us, the reader, a rhetorical question; don't we, ourselves, try to avoid having something we fear confirmed and made real to us? **Throughout the novel, there are touches of psychological realism** like this, which try to offset the less than realistic elements of Pip's persistence in clinging to the romantic wreckage of his early aspirations for Estella. Dickens is taking trouble now to make Pip's emotions as realistic as possible; he remains fearful that something may happen to Magwitch, and is in "a state of constant restlessness and suspense", while he waits week after week for Wemmick to send a sign that he thinks it is safe to try to remove Magwitch abroad.

At the theatre, he finds Wopsle staring at him from the stage; he waits for him, and explains that he is sure that Compeyson had been sitting in the row behind Pip, "like a ghost", and had left before the end of the performance. Naturally, Pip feels "enhanced disquiet", and a "special and peculiar terror", because when Pip is watching the performance is the only time Compeyson is not in his thoughts. Compeyson was dressed, Wopsle says, "prosperously……in black". Pip writes to Wemmick, to make him aware that Compeyson is so close at hand.

Chapter 48

Dickens dares to use the same plot device again- another chance meeting leads to another discovery. Pip meets Jaggers in the street, and he insists that Pip comes to his house that evening to join him and Wemmick for a meal. Pip accepts, only because he wants to see Wemmick. But Wemmick behaves to Pip "as dry and distant…..as if there were twin Wemmicks and this was the wrong one"; he has his Little Britain personality, not his "Walworth sentiments", and takes the distinction so far as to look only at Jaggers, and ignore Pip.

Miss Havisham has sent a short note asking Pip to visit her, to resolve Pip's request that she should take on his financial commitment to Herbert.

Jaggers then confirms, quite bluntly, that Drummle "has won the pool" (or scooped the lottery) and married Estella. Jaggers offers his assessment of the couple- that Estella is more intelligent, but that he may have the upper hand "if he should…beat her" (we know that Drummle is capable of violence, because he throws glasses when he is angry; he had almost done so during the dinner Jaggers had hosted in Chapter 27). Jaggers says that someone of Drummle's type "either beats, or cringes"; he will either dominate or be dominated, and in such a trial of strength he hopes that Estella will prevail.

Molly is waiting on them, and now "the action of her fingers…like the action of knitting", and her "attentive eyes", give Dickens the opportunity to make Pip link her with Estella, as he sees her as the embodiment of how Estella will look after twenty years of being beaten, "of a brutal husband and a stormy life". It is not a happy picture!

Pip looks back at the "inexplicable feeling" he had had, several times, that Estella reminded him of someone. And so what he knew was true in his subconscious mind becomes clear to his conscious mind- just as he half-knows that Drummle will beat Estella, that Miss Havisham will die, and that Magwitch will be captured.

Along with the revelation that Estella is married, therefore, comes the certainty, for Pip, "that this woman was Estella's mother". This, of course, leads to a separate question; who is her father? Pip is indeed an orphan; Estella has been brought up as if she is one; but both of her parents are alive, and close at hand.

Jaggers acknowledges the sensitivity, for Pip, of the subject of Estella's marriage. The answer, for Jaggers, is not to commiserate, or discuss it, but to be convivial, and pass the wine around again.

Pip and Wemmick "leave early", and, as soon as he is outside, Wemmick drops his stiffness, and is able to feel "unscrewed" or uninhibited. Pip asks him how Jaggers had turned Molly into "a wild beast tamed"; Wemmick says that "that's **his secret**".

His hold over her came from his success in having Molly acquitted of murder; the case made his reputation as an advocate, because it was "desperate", and there were no other suspects. By tampering with the evidence, by ignoring the strength in her wrists (which he now makes a point of demonstrating), by dressing her at her trial so that "she looked much slighter than she really was", and by telling the prosecution that they should perhaps have charged her with infanticide first, he put the jury in a position where "they gave in". To use Jaggers' own language, he beat them, verbally, and they cringed.

Molly, saved by Jaggers, went to work for him immediately, and "was tamed from the beginning". As he has shown no propensity for violence, or for losing his self-control, it seems likely that Jaggers' power over Molly arises from his intellectual superiority and her obligation to him; no-one in the novel can stand up to him. When Pip first met him, he somehow gave the impression he has **secret knowledge of everyone** which he could use against them if he so wishes (Chapters 18, 20) and he has the power of making even the innocent feel guilty (Chapter 36). But how different from Drummle's desire to dominate through violence is Jaggers' performance as a legal professional? Jaggers certainly embodies the will to win. In leaving his house unlocked, and challenging the criminal community to dare to burgle him, he out-spiders the Spider, Drummle; he is like a judicial "man-trap", and would "have the lives" of any who robbed him ("he'd have all he could get…...they dread him….he's artful", as Wemmick says in chapter 25).

Wemmick confirms to Pip that Molly's child, whom she may or may not have "frantically destroyed", was a girl (this is, of course, Estella). Pip can now add the new worry about how Drummle will treat Estella to his familiar anxiety about Magwitch and Compeyson.

Chapter 49

This is a long chapter in which Pip and Miss Havisham meet, she sees the very regrettable (though unintended) consequences of her self-indulgent behaviour, she asks him to forgive her, and she is mortally injured in the fire.

The second paragraph sets the scene in religious terms (the old monks, the cathedral chimes, funeral music, the priory-garden) and associates the absence of Estella from Satis House with desolation. Miss Havisham is suddenly alone; Pip is her confessor, and she seeks forgiveness before her fatal illness arises out of her accident.

Dickens was writing a century and a half go, and we live today in a society which is, broadly, more secular. **We are less sympathetic to the idea that we need to be cleansed of sin before we die**; this isn't Dickens' fault. In reading this chapter, we should bear in mind that it may well have had a moral seriousness for readers in Dickens' own time which has become diluted since.

Miss Havisham is staring into the fire, and has "an air of utter loneliness upon her". She seems afraid of Pip, just as she had seemed afraid of Estella; this is because her span of control has weakened. In order to be- in Jaggers' terms- a "beater" (and certainly one who growled too), she had suppressed any compassion or human feeling, but now she cannot, and she has become a "cringer". She wants to show Pip that she is "not all stone", so she provides the £900 for Herbert, and offers to help Pip financially. She thinks that he must hate her. She develops, in her way of speaking to Pip, "an unwonted tone of sympathy"; and she feels too guilty to look at him.

When Pip affirms that he can forgive her any wrongs she has done him, here and now, because "my life has been a blind and thankless one; and I want forgiveness and direction", he is showing a human sympathy and tolerance which reduces her to the posture and behaviour of a beggar, a supplicant or a worshipper.

She, like Jaggers, confirms the awful truth to Pip, that Estella is married (he already knew this, because he could sense the "new desolation in the desolate house"). **Pip's response to her repeated rhetorical exclamation "What have I done!" is that she was wrong to shape Estella in the negative way she did; but more wrong in refusing to move on from her own disappointment and betrayal, because that sort of development and personal growth is "the appointed order of (the) Maker". Her behaviour is, Pip judges, a collection of "monstrous vanities",** and she is out of place, because of "her profound unfitness for this earth".

It is observing the depth of Pip's suffering which has brought back to Miss Havisham the real meaning of her own. Pip points out to her that, rather than lamenting her actions, she should try to restore to Estella what she has "done amiss in keeping a part of her right nature away from her" (remember Pip's discussions with Biddy about what is natural or in human nature). Miss Havisham, by her own admission, has "stole(n) her heart away and put ice in its place". When Jaggers brought Estella; and she originally merely "wanted a little girl to rear and love, and save from my fate".

Pip walks round the garden because he has a premonition ("a presentiment") that this is his last visit, and that "the dying light" is apt (he will visit the site again in Chapter 59, but the house will have been demolished). His vision of Miss Havisham, dead, and hanging from a beam in the brewery, makes him shudder from head to foot; so he returns to check that she is safe, discovers the fire, and saves her from it.

In doing so, he pulls down the table cloth, and the cake ("the heap of rottenness…. and all the ugly things that sheltered there"). The disturbing of the deathly environment she has created is a form of redemptive destruction for Miss Havisham (as is the fire which cripples Rochester in "Jane Eyre"). Pip holds her "forcibly down with all my strength, like a prisoner who might escape". Miss Havisham is undergoing what we might describe as an exorcism. When what Joe Gargery might have called 'the evil in her heart' is expelled, there is no life force left.

Pip is burnt, but Miss Havisham is in a state of shock. Her bed is put on the table, where she lies, as she had predicted she would; and, although the ancient wedding dress has been burnt, she is covered with cotton wool and a white sheet. This is also reminiscent of Arthur Havisham's shroud in Chapter 42; now, she has "the phantom air of something that had been and was changed".

That night, **her speech becomes an incoherent incantation of three phrases- "What have I done!", "I meant to save her from misery like mine", and "Take the pencil and write under my name, "I forgive her!"- and sometimes she leaves a word out. This is precisely the same pattern of speech that Biddy reported that Mrs Joe had used in her dying moments (in Chapter 35)- "she presently said "Joe" again, and once "Pardon", and once "Pip"….and it was just an hour later when…….we found she was gone".** When Pip leaves next morning, and gives her a light kiss, Miss Havisham is still repeating her desire to be forgiven.

Summary Chapters 46-49

After detaching himself from the emotionless world of Satis House, Pip's meeting Clara Barley, and the deep, uncomplicated and caring attachment he observes between Herbert and her, reinforces our sense that he is excluded from romantic happiness – at least, for now. His "expectations" have made him responsible not for Estella but for Magwitch. Clara's respectful and accommodating approach to her unreasonable father may be teaching Pip to tolerate and accept the whims of his own pseudo-father, Magwitch.

Certainly, the qualities she shows of being "gentle" and "needing protection", and which strike Pip, apply equally, now, to Magwitch. Where Pip at first loathed him (Chapter 40), now he is "anxious at parting from him". He thinks, too, of his "very sad" parting from Estella. Pip is "dispirited". While Herbert's thoughts are optimistic, Pip has a premonition that the tide of the river is bringing his pursuers towards Magwitch, "swiftly, silently, and surely"- which is precisely what Compeyson is doing.

Pip's life is "unhappy", restless, anxious; he waits, inactive, for the signal from Wemmick to move Magwitch down the Thames to safety. Pip's visit to see Wopsle's latest performance confirms that Compeyson is worryingly nearby, "sitting behind….like a ghost".

Jaggers passes on Miss Havisham's message, that Pip should visit her again, to resolve his request that she could help Herbert financially (now that he has dissociated himself from his own/ Magwitch's fortune). The dinner at Jaggers' house enables Pip to make the association between Estella's hands and Molly's, then their hair and their eyes. He knows that Molly is Estella's mother. This leaves just one question unresolved; who is her father?

Pip reminds Wemmick that he had described Molly as "a wild beast tamed". This links with Jaggers' speculation on who will emerge on top, in the marriage of the "beater" Drummle; will he "growl", and will Estella "cringe"? Wemmick now tells Pip about Jaggers' personal connection with Estella (whom he had saved from a criminal background, and entrusted to the care of Miss Havisham). Estella is certainly wild, and seems unlikely to be tamed.

Pip's final visit to Miss Havisham is preceded by cathedral bells which sound to him like "funeral music". She, like Magwitch, is about to suffer near-fatal injuries in an accident; Pip is present at both of the incidents which, in effect, orphan Estella (as she does not know her own mother) and make her his equal in that sense.

Pip feels compassion for Miss Havisham in her "utter loneliness". She is now apprehensive, and seems afraid of him; the locus of power in their relationship has turned, and, now, she is the child, and Pip is the parent. She wants to right the wrongs she has done to him, and asks Pip to forgive her.

He is less concerned about the wrongs done to him than about the "vanity" which has led her to ruin her own powers of recovery, and Estella's power to love (the power which Pip wanted to be directed at him by Estella, but not by the infinitely more deserving Biddy). Miss Havisham's intention was to "save (Estella) from my fate"; but, in saving her from suffering a broken heart, she has made her cruel, and an agent of suffering.

Pip walks in the garden, in the "dying light", and feels a premonition of Miss Havisham's death; his return to the house enables him to save her from the fire, while he is injured himself. Her wedding dress is burnt, but she is laid on the table (as she predicted she would be) in a sheet which is like a shroud. The power of premonition- hers, and Pip's- lends more credence to our fears that Pip's intuition, that disaster awaits Magwitch, must also be true.

Chapter 50

Herbert is attending to Pip's burns, which have to be dressed regularly. He needs to recover swiftly, so that their opportunity to row Magwitch down the river Thames is not affected by a long delay.

Herbert tells Pip that Magwitch has talked to him about the "woman that he had had great trouble with", (which turns out to be Molly) and the detail of his account of those years, her trial for the murder of the woman found throttled in the barn, and her acquittal, thanks to Jaggers, all match Wemmick's account of the episode to Pip in Chapter 48.

Magwitch believes that Molly had carried out her threat to kill their child. Being reluctant to testify if she were to be tried for that crime, he kept out of the way of the murder trial, and lost any contact with her immediately afterwards (when she went straight to work for Jaggers). This was just after Compeyson had started to use Magwitch as his junior partner in crime, and, according to Herbert, he then "used the knowledge.....as a means of keeping him poorer, and working him harder". Magwitch could be -effectively- blackmailed by Compeyson, who could have gone to the police with the accusation that Molly had killed their daughter.

Pip knows that Jaggers presented the child as an orphan to Miss Havisham. That, and Molly's trial, had taken place twenty years ago, and three or four years before Pip first met Magwitch in the graveyard. So **the information that Estella's mother was Magwitch's wife proves conclusively that he is Estella's father.**

If Drummle had known that Estella's parents were an unconvicted murderess and a transported career criminal, he would not have married her. If Magwitch had known that Estella was alive, he would have passed his fortune on to her, rather than Pip.

Estella has become gentrified, and has taken her place in respectable society, in the way Pip had hoped to himself, although Miss Havisham's is "old money" and Pip's, from Magwitch, is "new money". Estella (like Daisy Buchanan in F Scott Fitzgerald's "The Great Gatsby") has married into old money (Drummle's) where she is bound to be brutalised and unhappy. Pip (like Jay Gatsby) remains an outsider because his origins are dubious; because he has been unable to save Estella from a socially respectable but otherwise disastrous marriage; and because, in Pip's own mind, Magwitch's fortune is tainted.

It is interesting that, **in some ways, Jaggers is responsible for these secrets and lies. He helped Molly to evade justice (and death); he knew that Estella was not really an orphan, but thought that, in giving her to Miss Havisham, he was protecting her from a worse life. Also, he did not disclose to Pip that Magwitch was his benefactor, but left Pip to the uncertainty and speculation which has led him to suffer.**

Molly's secret will be revealed, now that Pip knows it; Magwitch will be revealed, now that Compeyson is so close to finding him.

Keeping secrets yields power over those who hide them, to those who know them- the power Jaggers has over Molly is similar to the power Compeyson had over Magwitch.

I think that the concepts of corruptibility, and of unintended consequences, are more important to Dickens in this novel than a narrower focus on criminality. Jaggers does what he can to save his clients (including both Magwitch and Molly), but the true cost of doing so is that hiding the truth beneath a cloak of practicality leaves longer-term problems. Miss Havisham set out to protect Estella, but turned her into the equivalent of Frankenstein's monster- a being with too much power to harm others and too little empathy.

Now it is Pip's turn to try to protect Magwitch by hiding him. Just as Jaggers has protected him (by hiding his return to England) and Molly (by perverting the evidence at her trial twenty years ago- his admiration of the strength in her wrists means she *did* commit the murder) because to betray them, or reveal the truth, would condemn them to death, Pip is trying to keep Magwitch safe from a death sentence. But **secrets will come out**- and so the revelations of these last few chapters (especially Chapters 42, 48 and this one, 50) give us **the sense that the attempt to save Magwitch must be bound to fail, because Jaggers' saving people never really solves the underlying issues, and neither did Miss Havisham's mission to save Estella from her own fate.** (Marrying Drummle may in fact be worse than being abandoned at the altar.)

We have an underlying sense that, just as Pip's help could not save Magwitch from being recaptured on the marshes, his capacity to guarantee his safety is, again, far from absolute now.

Chapter 51

Pip wants Jaggers to confirm his understanding of Estella's history and parentage; his sense of loyalty and of his duty of care towards Magwitch can only be made stronger as a result (adding more dramatic tension to the plot).

Again, Jaggers uses the hypothetical, to frame the truth ("Put the case that a woman………I'll put a case to you. Mind! I admit nothing."), as if he were in a court of law, and incriminating himself. He himself has not realised until now that Magwitch is Estella's father. Despite his professional manner of speech, Jaggers' account of his motive in passing Estella to Miss Havisham is moving- he has often seen "children solemnly tried at a criminal bar…..imprisoned, whipped, transported, neglected, cast out…….and growing up to be hanged".

Estella could be saved from a life of crime, and, by giving her to Miss Havisham, Jaggers could ensure her safety even if Molly were found guilty and executed. Molly was then so terrorised by her trial that "she was scared out of the ways of the world" and had no desire to care for her own child.

This rather reluctant piece of self-justification by Jaggers comes with an element of comedy, in the way in which he tries to hide his surprise at hearing that Magwitch is Estella's father, and his complete unawareness that Wemmick has "an old father, and…pleasant and playful ways".

Jaggers and Wemmick both suggest that Pip should have accepted Miss Havisham's offer of financial help for himself as well as Herbert (portable property, once more). **Pip, however, simply wants "assurance of the truth"- that Jaggers took Estella from Molly and gave her to Miss Havisham. Pip's superior knowledge here inverts his usual relationship with Jaggers- it is as if Pip is the lawyer, and Jaggers the defendant**. Pip encourages disclosure on the basis that "I said that I did not blame him, or suspect him, or mistrust him"; we can accept that Jaggers' original motive, to save just one child from "an atmosphere of evil", was good. Among all the ambivalent things Jaggers does in his professional life- exploiting the weakness of the legal system for money- *there is this one shining good deed*. It is Jaggers' equivalent of Pip's financial support for Herbert.

The last part of the chapter has **Jaggers advising Pip to keep the secret** he has found out. He cannot see that either Molly or Magwitch would benefit from knowing of the other's nearness. Revealing the truth would "drag" Estella "back to disgrace" because Drummle would reject her. Memorably, he suggests that Pip would be better off cutting his own hands off than disturbing the way things are for the three people concerned.

Wemmick and Jaggers are both uncomfortable that they have revealed to each other that they have a personal, as well as a professional side. Because the business of the law cannot be complicated by emotion, they join forces to eject the unfortunate, snivelling Mike, whose daughter has been arrested for shoplifting, because they will "have no feelings here".

Chapter 52

Miss Havisham's £900 enables Herbert to become a partner in Clarriker's, the firm he is working at. A new office will be set up, abroad ("in the East") and Herbert will run it.

One Monday in March, Wemmick sends a letter advising Pip to move Magwitch that Wednesday. Pip is still too injured to row, but Startop can help. The important point is to get Magwitch at least "well beyond Gravesend, which was a critical place for search or enquiry if suspicion were afoot". Once there, they can wait quietly for a ship bound for any European port. They make the necessary plans within a few hours.

But Pip then finds, at home, "a very dirty letter", demanding that he comes -alone- that night or the following night, to the sluice-house on the marshes next to the lime-kiln, to be given "information regarding your uncle Provis". Because of the time it takes the coach, Pip makes an instant decision to go; he leaves a misleading note for Herbert, saying he is going to see Miss Havisham. He is flustered, and unsure of the wisdom of going, but he is afraid that, if he does not, Magwitch's escape could be prevented.

There is a clue to the possible author of the letter, buried in Chapter 15- "he (Orlick) lodged at a sluice-keeper's out on the marshes", but it would be a very sharp reader who identifies "sluice-house" with Orlick.

Pip stays "at an inn of minor reputation down the town", where the landlord has to help him by cutting up his food, and regales Pip with Pumblechook's version of Pip's own history- that Pumblechook had "done everything for him" (facilitating the relationship with Miss Havisham which enabled his fortune) but that Pip "gives the cold shoulder to the man that made him". Pip is struck that, while Pumblechook complains about Pip's neglect of his old associates, Joe, who has cause to, does not. Pip feels "humbled" by Joe's nobility, and dejected and remorseful about his own behaviour; but he has to go to meet the author of the anonymous letter. He has dropped the letter itself- he presumes, in the coach.

Chapter 53

The description of the isolated kiln and the fragile old wooden sluice-house, on a dark, "dismal" night, "melancholy........oppressive" takes a page, and sets the scene for the drama which follows. Rather like Goldilocks at the cottage of the three bears, Pip sees a light inside; knocks on the door, twice; and then goes inside. There are signs of habitation, including a lighted candle on the table; after a few moments of suspense, Pip is "caught in a strong running noose thrown over my head from behind". Here is yet another threat of death by hanging!

Because Pip has lived to tell the tale (he is narrating the novel), we know that he survives this attack; we are more interested in who the attacker is, and why they are doing this to him. Pip's ability to resist his attacker is poor, because of his burns, which are painful. When his attacker eventually succeeds in striking a light, Pip is surprised to see Orlick.

Orlick calls Pip "you enemy", and he declares that he is going to kill Pip when he is ready. He has kept the gun he had, as the gatekeeper at Miss Havisham's - the job from which Jaggers sacked him, because Pip said he was unsuitable. He accuses Pip, too, of daring "to come betwixt me and a young woman I liked"- presumably Biddy. Orlick has also memorised Pip's comment that he would "take any pains, and spend any money, to drive me out of this country"- the remark Pip made in Chapter 35 when Biddy felt that Orlick was stalking them. Moreover, Orlick resents "all" Pip's money; and he confesses to murdering Mrs Joe ("your shrew sister"), for which he blames Pip, who, he says, allowed Mrs Joe to favour him while Orlick himself was "bullied and beat". The murder weapon- which he has kept, intending to kill Pip with it too- is Magwitch's old leg-iron.

Orlick tells Pip that he plans to kill him, and dispose of the evidence by putting his body in the lime-kiln. The suddenness of the threat, and the apparent impossibility of escaping, leaves Pip facing a terrible, imminent death, "but far more terrible than death was the dread of being misremembered after death". He resolves not to beg Orlick to spare him, but feels "a scornful detestation of him that sealed my lips". Pip felt the same desire- to be remembered fondly after his own death- on the day of his sister's funeral (Chapter 35).

Lastly, Orlick confirms that he was the "lurker on the stairs", because he was trying to find a way to plot how to kill Pip; and in doing so, he accidentally discovered "your uncle Provis". He is working for Compeyson; Compeyson wrote the letter, to lure Pip here, and Compeyson knows that Magwitch's return to England represents a threat to him.

Pip realises that, once Orlick has completed this explanation, and finished his bottle of spirits, he is ready to kill him with "a stone-hammer with a long heavy handle". As Pip fights him off, his rescuers arrive, and Orlick runs away. The rescuers are Trabb's boy (to whom Pip gives two guineas, much as Magwitch had sent him the two pounds), Herbert and Startop.

Pip had dropped the letter not in the coach but at home. Herbert and Startop had followed him, and Trabb had guided them to the sluice-house. **They leave the question of having Orlick arrested, fearing that any more delays will make it even harder for Magwitch to get away. Perhaps this is a mistake, but it is necessary in order to bring the plot to its dramatic climax; arresting Orlick would surely lead to the arrest of Compeyson too, and guarantee Magwitch's safety, but that is not the ending for the novel that Dickens has in mind!**

They get back to London after dawn, and Pip spends Tuesday in bed, recovering from the assault, and feeling anxious and fretful, in case he is too unwell to carry out the plan on Wednesday. But, next day, he feels "strong and well". Herbert, too, is cheerful and optimistic. But he had not heard Orlick's last words- " **'Ware Compeyson, Magwitch, and the gallows!"**

Orlick's malevolence towards Pip is as animalistic and primitive as Magwitch's towards Compeyson (and Compeyson's towards Magwitch). The (successful) struggle from which Pip escapes, wounded but well, foreshadows the struggle from which Magwitch will emerge, his mortal enemy dead, but himself wounded and fated to die.

This is the material of epic poetry and heroic saga, and perhaps it is the mixture of this life and death conflict with the romanticism and fantasy of Pip's earlier imaginative and emotional life which makes the novel "tragi-comic", as Dickens called it. As we move towards the final drama, the narrative is gathering speed, and there is no time any more for the slower pace of the comic episodes.

Summary Chapters 50-53

Magwitch has told Herbert the story of his marriage, Molly's trial, and her threat to kill their child (Estella). Because Pip has understood the resemblance between Molly and Estella, this proves that Magwitch is her father.

Pip goes to Little Britain, to obtain Miss Havisham's cheque for £900, to support Herbert, secretly; and to ask Jaggers what he knows about Estella. Jaggers is caught off guard, for once; he has no idea that she is Magwitch's daughter, the child of two of his former clients. When Pip asks Wemmick to endorse his appeal to Jaggers, on account of Wemmick's own capacity for emotion, Jaggers becomes less dispassionate and self-contained, and explains how and why he saved Estella, and passed her on from Molly to Miss Havisham, because her father "believed her dead, and dared make no stir about". To the reader, it is clear that, in the same way Pip has used his expectations to enable Herbert to achieve his own independence, Jaggers had saved Estella from "growing up to be hanged". Magwitch and Miss Havisham, too, commit a single, significant act of generosity, to help Pip and Herbert respectively.

Jaggers advises Pip that it is in no-one's interest to reveal Estella's true parentage; he suggests, comically/grotesquely, that Pip might as well cut his own hands off, for all the good it would do to reveal the truth. In a moment which combines rich humour with true pathos, Jaggers and Wemmick divert themselves from the emotional vulnerability they have each just revealed by telling Mike Spooney not to be so emotive about his eldest daughter's arrest for shoplifting- "I'll have no feelings here. Get out."

Wemmick sends Pip a note signalling that it is a good time to move Magwitch. Later, we come to know that Compeyson has deceived Wemmick too. But the preparation is disrupted by the anonymous letter Pip receives, demanding he goes to the sluice-house on the marshes, alone, for "information" about "your uncle Provis". This is Orlick's revenge; just like the murder of Mrs Joe, and Magwitch's return, it proves, regarding Pip, that- to coin a phrase- you can take the boy out of the marshes, but you can't take the marshes out of the boy.

Pip reflects on the goodness of Joe and Biddy, and the vanity of Pumblechook. Then he sets out for the marshes, where Orlick tries to kill him. Orlick resents Pip's friendship with Biddy, his preferential status as Joe's apprentice, and the fact that Pip had him sacked from the position of armed doorman at Satis House. Pip fears his own apparently inevitable death less than "being misremembered after death". Orlick's resentment of Pip is the resentment of one with no advantages towards one with some. In this, it resembles Magwitch's towards Compeyson. Orlick's is wrong; Magwitch's is right. The world of justice, of motive, of innocence and guilt, is more complex than we may think.

Chapter 54

This is a long chapter, and a masterclass in the control of pace and drama. It spans from 8.30 on Tuesday morning to late afternoon on Wednesday, by which time the escape has failed, Magwitch faces a death sentence, and Compeyson has drowned.

The plan is to row with the tide until 3pm, and then against it until dusk, by when they will have passed Gravesend and reached desolate countryside where they can wait overnight for a steamer to Hamburg or Rotterdam.

Pip feels "freshened with new hope", but he is not the most prominent character here. Apart from describing the river Thames and the activity on it with great detail, Dickens concentrates on Magwitch, whom we have barely seen since Chapter 42.

Magwitch "was the least anxious of any of us". Having originally hoped to see Pip as a fine "brought-up London gentleman" (Chapter 39), he now "hoped to live to see his gentleman one of the best of gentleman in a foreign country"; at the end of this chapter, that hope has gone, and he reflects "I've seen my boy, and he can be a gentleman without me". **Pip knows (as do Jaggers and Wemmick) that once Magwitch is convicted, "his possessions would be forfeited to the Crown"; Magwitch is unaware of that legal ramification.** The arresting officer takes possession "of everything the prisoner had about him", including the pocket-book.

On the outward journey, Magwitch explains to Pip that being able to sit with Pip, and smoke, is all the more precious to someone who has spent most of their life imprisoned. Pip understands that, for Magwitch, freedom and danger go together, because he is always being hunted (by the end of this chapter, he is "the hunted wounded shackled creature"). When he was in Australia, his life became "flat" or dull and unsatisfying (just as Estella marries Drummle out of boredom).

With a **grimly prophetic irony**, when Pip asks him whether he thinks he will be safe in a few hours' time, **Magwitch says "we can no more see to the bottom of the next few hours, than we can see to the bottom of this river".** He is not "passive or resigned", or "despondent", but is "composed and contented", though he is starting to feel "a trifle old".

The journey appears to pass without alarm, and by evening they have made good progress to the desolate marshland, where "all about us was stagnation and mud". At sunset, they are nervous again about any noise they hear (just as Magwitch had explained in Chapter 3, the smallest noise on the marshes is alarming, when you are escaping, and fear you are being followed); they find a grubby pub to stay at overnight, where there is only the landlord, his wife, and a "Jack", or odd-job man, who retrieves the bodies of those who have drowned, and wears their clothes.

He has seen "a four-oared galley" on that stretch of the river, with "two sitters"; he thinks it is the (hated) customs officers, the landlord disagrees, and Pip and the others feel "uneasy"; he feels "that we were caged and threatened", and when he wakes up during the night he sees two men inspecting their boat, which implies that they are being watched. It turns out, the next day, that the "sitters" are Compeyson and a river police officer.

Magwitch, meanwhile, remains "the least anxious of the party", and thinks the galley is the customs officers', and nothing sinister. He has tended to underestimate the danger he is in, ever since he first revealed himself to Pip.

The one o'clock steamer is late, so that two large boats arrive together "at full speed"; at the critical moment. The four-oared galley "shoot(s) out from under the bank", and seeks to arrest Magwitch; it rams the rowing boat, and the water displaced by the Hamburg steamer, together with Magwitch's lunge towards Compeyson, capsizes the boat. Magwitch resurfaces, able to swim, but with "some very severe injury in the chest and a deep cut in the head"; he is then "manacled at the wrists and the ankles". He had had a struggle underwater with Compeyson, who has not reappeared, and must have drowned.

Magwitch is now a condemned man. Pip decides that being with him "was my place henceforth while he lived"; he holds his hand; and the old "repugnance to him had all melted away" because Pip realises that Magwitch- his surrogate father- has been more generous and loyal to him than Pip has been to Joe, his step-father and companion. Poignantly, Pip knows that it is preferable if Magwitch's injuries are fatal, to save him from being executed publicly.

They complete the journey back to London on the police boat, against the background of "the setting sun…and as the stream of our hopes seemed all running back"; Magwitch remains "quite content", although his prediction that time, like the river, is dark and unfathomable, has been proved correct in the most awful way.

Magwitch says that it is better for Pip, "as a gentleman", not to be associated with him any more; his only request is that he visits him in prison when Wemmick does, and that he sits in the gallery when he is tried and sentenced "for the last o' many times". Pip is determined to be with Magwitch as much as he is allowed, but, out of compassion, he will allow him to persist in the misconception that Pip will still have his money- "he need never know how his hopes of enriching me had perished".

Even in this crucial chapter, Compeyson has a non-speaking role. He has been spoken about- particularly when Magwitch recounted their dealings, in Chapter 42- and he spoke for himself, very briefly, when he and Magwitch were recaptured, in Chapter 5, but only to accuse Magwitch, three times, of trying to murder him. **Compeyson must be one of the most economically characterised villains in the world of novels!**

Chapter 55

Pip engages Jaggers again, as Magwitch's defence lawyer. He says that Magwitch's case is hopeless, and is "querulous and angry" with Pip for letting Magwitch's fortune go. Because Pip is not a relative of Magwitch's, and in the absence of a legal settlement of the money on him, the State will take it. Pip decides that he will not attempt to claim that Magwitch's money should pass to him on his death. Magwitch wrongly assumes that everything he owns will become Pip's.

Compeyson had been carrying documents which showed that he knew a good deal about what Magwitch owned. He also deceived Wemmick, via the information he received from prisoners in Newgate, into believing that he had gone away at the very time Wemmick therefore suggested it was safe for Magwitch to escape. Wemmick believes that Compeyson was so determined that Magwitch could not have been saved; but his "portable property" should have been. Although Wemmick expresses his sadness ("I haven't been so cut up for a long time") it is a very unsentimental and controlled sadness- presumably because he sees petty criminals being condemned to death all the time.

Magwitch faces a trial a month later; this is a narrative choice which allows Dickens to develop the relationship between him and Pip further. Meanwhile, Herbert has to go to Cairo to set up his new shipping office; he offers Pip a job as a clerk there, living with him and Clara once they are married. This would be reminiscent of the old life, where Pip, as a young teenager, lived with Joe and Mrs Joe as Joe's apprentice; **Pip's future is beginning to resemble the past he had left behind**. But he says he cannot take in the offer, and "there was a vague something lingering in my thoughts"- his rather presumptuous idea that Biddy might now be willing to marry him, as we will soon discover.

Clara is still tied to her father's care, but he will soon die, and she will then be free to go abroad; again, this mirrors Pip's position. All Pip has now is his tie to the dying Magwitch, and a "lonely home" which does not seem a home at all.

Wemmick asks Pip to "take a walk" with him the following Monday, and the narrative goes straight on to that day. Wemmick has, in fact, arranged his own wedding to Miss Skiffins and wants Pip to be his "backer, or best-man". The only other guest, bar one "pew opener", is the Aged P. The service is depicted comically, with the front of the church described as "those fatal rails", and a physical struggle to get the Aged's gloves on to his hands. Wemmick, conscious that Jaggers may think that he is "softening", asks Pip to keep the wedding secret from him!

The fact that Wemmick is married, and Herbert is about to be, reinforces our sense of Pip's isolation and loneliness; his infatuation with Estella has prevented him from forming a serious relationship of his own. We are reminded of Pip's conversation with Herbert in Chapter 30; Pip had thought he was "very lucky", but Herbert had foreseen "miserable things" in Pip's infatuation with Estella, and had asked him to try to "detach" himself from those thoughts and feelings. Despite his financial poverty, Herbert is in a better position emotionally and regarding his prospects than Pip has ever been. And, **once Joe and Biddy are married, the frequency of church bells will be as great as in a romantic novel or a Shakespeare comedy, apart from the fact that Pip, whose expectations were so great, is left entirely alone.**

Chapter 56

Magwitch is kept in the prison hospital and his injuries are making him "slowly weaker and worse"; he seems "tired out", and resigned to his fate. Pip occasionally wonders whether Magwitch thinks that, if his circumstances in life had been better, he would had a better life; but he never indulges in complaining, regret or self-pity, and that quiet nobility has influenced Pip to some degree.

Jaggers applies for the trial to be postponed (in the hope that Magwitch will not live long enough to attend it) but is refused. The trial and the sentencing (with Pip holding Magwitch's hand) are, for Pip, a "terrible experience". Dickens makes Magwitch one of no fewer than thirty-two convicts who are sentenced to death. He manages our sympathies here very carefully and effectively. **The judgment is narrated in indirect speech, so that the theatricality of the scene is played down and the horror played up. It is crushing, dispassionate and unfeeling.**

The judge who condemns them, and the thirty-two people he is condemning, are caught in a single shaft of sunlight. **The narrative suggests that, despite the power of the law, all of us are "passing on, with absolute equality, to the greater Judgment that knoweth all things and cannot err". I take this scene as an argument in favour of abolishing the death penalty for the offences it was being used for in Dickens' own time.**

Pip is in the difficult position of hoping that Magwitch will die before he can be executed; he writes to the Home Secretary and to the Queen, appealing for clemency (there is a deafening silence; there will be no happy ending here). But Magwitch does become more and more ill, and less able to speak. He praises Pip for his loyalty and constancy ("You've never deserted me, dear boy") - but Pip knows, as we do, that he had intended to run away and abandon him when he first returned. Then he becomes unable to speak, but he understands when Pip confirms to him that Estella is alive, "a lady and very beautiful. And I love her!" (Magwitch had no idea that the "bright eyes" which he had thought animated Pip's behaviour were Estella's).

Summary Chapters 54-56

These chapters cover Magwitch's planned escape, his capture and death. Magwitch behaves without anxiety or self-pity. He is a hunted animal, but he has a nobility which sets him apart from all the other characters, and which we would not expect to encounter in a career criminal.

Dickens prepares for the dramatic climax of Magwitch's capture with the talk of the four-oared galley in the pub downriver, and with Pip, awoken by the pub's sign creaking in the wind (like the gallows?), seeing two men looking at their boat in the middle of the night.

Magwitch and Compeyson are locked in a fight, just as they were in the ditch on the marshes, when they were recaptured. Compeyson is drowned, accidentally, and Magwitch's injuries will prove fatal; but not until Dickens has used them to dramatise the pathos of the way the death penalty is imposed on a variety of petty criminals.

Pip allows Magwitch to persist in the mistaken belief that his fortune will still pass to Pip (it will be forfeited to the Crown) - he has learnt that some secrets need to be kept, out of a sense of compassion, and to avoid causing distress. Pip is conscious that Magwitch has been "a much better man" to him than he has been himself to Joe.

In a neat reversal of the patron and the beneficiary, Herbert offers Pip a job as a clerk in his new office in Cairo. Pip cannot accept the offer until he has stood by Magwitch, and until he has resolved "a vague something lingering in my thoughts"- which turns out to be the misguided hope that Biddy will agree to marry him, and that, having lost all his expectations, he will be able to go back to where he came from.

Wemmick's wedding, and the prospect of Herbert's, reinforce the sense of Pip's emotional isolation. All of his care is directed towards Magwitch. The last thing he tells Magwitch, as he is dying, is that Estella is alive and well, *and that he loves her.*

We sense that Pip has learnt (from Magwitch) the value of integrity and loyalty. Magwitch accepts his fate, and does not wish that he had had a different life to live. He suffers, but does not blame other people for his suffering. Pip has grown out of the romantic and unrealistic expectations of his younger self, and of London. He had hoped for "the best of everything" (Chapter 20) but none of his dreams have been realised. He has no money, once more; and he needs to put things right with Joe.

Chapter 57

As the process of tying up the loose ends in the novel continues, Pip now develops a stress-related illness. This is plausible enough, in the sense that his own injuries in the fire, plus his acute debts, plus the strain of what he has experienced with Magwitch, justify a delayed reaction; but the delirium which enables Dickens to bring Joe back as the person who is looking after Pip during this illness is very convenient for the narrative.

Debt collectors come to arrest Pip over an unpaid jeweller's bill, for £124, but he is too ill for them to take him away. When he regains proper consciousness and recognises Joe, Pip is struck, again, by his own ingratitude, and **he calls Joe "this gentle Christian man"- an interesting variation on the concept of a "gentleman".**

I find overtones here of the parable of the Prodigal Son in the New Testament (St Luke, 15:11-32). There, a man has two sons. The younger demands his share of the family estate, takes it, sets off for a distant land, and spends all he has received on wild living. Penniless and starving, he goes back to his family, repentant of his greed and stupidity, and he asks to be given a job as a servant. His father will not hear of it, but celebrates the return of his son, who was (metaphorically) dead and is alive again; was lost and is found.

It is through his materialistic adventure in the foreign land of London, and through losing his wealth, that Pip has learnt the true value of family ties, and recovered his humility.

Joe remains comical, in his speech (he is still mangling words), in his effortful writing to Biddy, and his circumlocution (he will not confirm that Miss Havisham is dead – "I wouldn't go so far as to say that"- but concedes that "she ain't living"). Equally, he will not say in so many words that Magwitch is dead- only that "I think as I did hear tell that how he were something or another in a general way in that direction". Joe's good nature will never give up on a cause, however dead it is!

Miss Havisham had altered her Will, to leave Matthew Pocket £4000, because of the good opinion Pip had given her of him, and just a pittance to Sarah, Camilla and Georgiana, because of their greed. Orlick, too, has, to some extent, been repaid for his wicked behaviour; he is now in prison, after breaking into Pumblechook's house.

In being the agent of some financial comfort for Matthew (as with Herbert) Pip feels that he has done something good. As his health gradually improves, he "fancied I was little Pip again". Meanwhile, Joe has sacked the corrupt old laundress (all servants in this novel are corrupt, apart from Trabb's boy) - proof, perhaps, that **money cannot buy affection or loyalty**.

Joe refuses to discuss Pip's change in fortunes, arguing that it is "unnecessary". Instead, he explains how he had felt ineffective in his attempts to save Pip from Tickler and Mrs Joe- "my power were not always fully equal to my inclinations"- but that he saw that when he tried to intervene it only made her more violent towards Pip. Joe puts a case (rather as Jaggers does, when he wants to explain himself without incriminating himself) that they should concentrate on "the good", and not on their past failings- or, by implication, Pip's neglect of Joe.

Partly because Pip has not been frank over the fact that he has no money at all (he does not want Joe to support him with his hard-earned savings), Joe becomes more formal and less familiar as Pip starts to recover his health; he must think that Pip will revert to his independent way of life. He leaves suddenly, "not wishful to intrude", and it is only now that Pip realises he has been kept out of prison for debt only because Joe had paid the outstanding bill.

Like the Prodigal Son, Pip intends to follow him "to the dear old forge…..(for) my penitent remonstrance with him". Pip also wants to show Biddy "how humbled and repentant I came back". He plans to ask her "to receive me like a forgiven child", resume their relationship, and to find a job in the country, work at the forge, or, if she agrees, he will take her to Cairo, where he will work for Herbert.

Pip is still being childish and childlike in his way of approaching a potential relationship. He seems aware of what it will provide for him (security, comfort) but less sure of- or interested in- what he can contribute to another person's happiness. **He has learned how to suffer, and he has learned how illusory the idea is that money brings happiness with it; but he has not yet learned to love.**

Chapter 58

Pip returns to the village via the Blue Boar; when he was last there, in Chapter 43, he had met Drummle, and he had realised that Estella was going to throw herself away on him; so staying there has become- for us, if not for him- a sign that Pip is about to receive an emotional blow.

The start of the chapter is humorous, as Pip narrates that, although he is now given a bedroom "among the pigeons and post-chaises", and treated less obsequiously, he sleeps just as well as when he was wealthy.

Before breakfast, he goes to Satis House, which is to be demolished, after its contents are auctioned. Then he meets Pumblechook, who claims that Pip's reversal in fortunes was inevitable- "What else could be expected!"- and stands over Pip as he eats a muffin, "staring fishily and breathing noisily, as he always did". Pumblechook shakes Pip's hand, as he had when Pip left for London, but now the action is less "servile"; he treats Pip as dissolute and immoral, and says that Pip has been brought low and "exhausted by the debilitating effects of prodigygality"- an amusing malapropism, confusing Pip the prodigal son with Pip the child prodigy in his acquiring wealth at such an early age.

Pumblechook's pomposity is amusing, but distressing for the reader too. He accuses Pip of lacking "gratitoode", and says that Joe is a man of "pig-headedness and ignorance". Pumblechook still maintains that he was Pip's "earliest benefactor" and that "Providence" has punished Pip for his "ingratitoode".

This set-piece lecture by Pumblechook, addressed to the staff at the pub, is a parody of the scene in which Jaggers held forth on the legal process, in the Jolly Bargemen, in Chapter 18.

The real business of this chapter is the return of the "prodigal" Pip to the forge, and to Biddy. Pip is physically weak, and walks there slowly, but he feels that, the nearer he gets to Joe and Biddy, the further away from "arrogance and untruthfulness" he is. The weather is "delicious", the sky blue, and the landscape "peaceful". Pip has tried to transfer his romantic fixation from Estella (something he had told Herbert it was impossible to do, in Chapter 30) to Biddy, but it remains self-centred- he imagines that, with Biddy as "a guiding spirit at my side", his character (and his perception of himself) will enjoy "change for the better". His feelings are very similar to, not just the prodigal son's, but those of Odysseus, who returned home, unrecognised, after many years fighting in the Trojan War, to resume his relationship with his wife Penelope-

"I felt like one who was toiling home barefoot from distant travel, and whose wanderings had lasted many years".

A narrative which deals with this theme of the wanderer returning home programmes us, as readers, to anticipate a happy ending, even though we are not sure what Pip will bring to a marriage to Biddy (just as we were unsure of what he would bring to Estella, beyond a cloying, idealistic devotion).

The narrative builds the suspense; Biddy's school is closed, and her house is too, and there is no sound of Joe's hammer coming from the forge. It is closed too. But the house is decorated with flowers, and Joe and Biddy are "arm in arm"- and just married, that same day.

It is the greatest improbability in the novel that Joe would re-marry without inviting Pip to the wedding, or letting him know. While Joe has shown how inferior he feels to Pip socially- and while Pip, conveniently for the plot, failed to explain to Joe how poor he had once again become, because of the forfeiture of Magwitch's assets- it is stretching credulity to suppose that he would not have informed Pip, at least.

In narrating the novel, Pip recalls that he had been within an hour of telling Joe about his own plans for Biddy. That would, of course, have forced the issue, and deprived Dickens **of the opportunity to dramatise a second experience for Pip of finding the woman on whom he had pinned his hopes committed to someone else without his knowledge**. It would also have soured Pip's relationship with Joe!

Pip now has no reason left to reject Herbert's offer of a job in Cairo, and he does have the motive that he wants to repay Joe for the money he had used to keep him out of the debtors' prison. **Pip** assesses his own behaviour as "thankless.........ungenerous and unjust", and he **asks Biddy and Joe to forgive him (just as Miss Havisham had pleaded with him to forgive her).**

Pip follows the same routine as he had when he left at the end of Chapter 19; only, then, Mrs Joe was alive, and Pip had gone to the finger-post alone, leaving Joe and Biddy in the house. The tone of this latest parting is **more sentimental but also more harmonious**.

<u>The next eleven years of Pip's adult life are disposed of in two paragraphs</u>- he and Herbert work happily and successfully, Herbert is married to Clara, Pip stays in touch with Joe and Biddy, and eventually Pip's good deed to Herbert is revealed (by Clarriker)- in keeping with the principle, in this novel, that **secrets cannot remain secret for ever**.

Chapter 59

Pip – now in his mid thirties - visits Joe, unannounced, one December; Joe and Biddy have a son, whom they have called Pip, and a daughter.

Biddy tells Pip that he should marry, but he thinks it is unlikely. She asks him whether he has "quite forgotten her"- meaning Estella. Pip says that, while he forgets none of his experiences, "that poor dream…has all gone by". Even as he says that, though, he knows that he will go back to Satis House that evening, to think of Estella.

Pip has heard that Estella was separated from Drummle, who had then died two years before the present time. When Pip makes his visit, "the stars were shining……and the evening was not dark". Sure enough, Estella is there too. **She too, like Magwitch, and like Pip, has been "softened" by her suffering- "I had never seen before….the saddened softened light of the once proud eyes", and her hand, previously "insensible", now has a "friendly touch".** That touch reminds Pip of what he had said to Magwitch, as Magwitch died, in Chapter 56; that Estella "is living now. She is a lady and very beautiful. And I love her". **The last of all the secrets in the novel is Pip's secret knowledge that Estella is Magwitch's daughter.**

Estella, like Pip, has lost everything- except for the ground on which Satis House had stood, and which is now to be built on again. She confesses that she has recently often thought of Pip, because she now appreciates his "worth", and that she has given the memory of their relationship " a place in my heart". Now Estella, like Pip, has "been bent and broken, but…….into a better shape", and she asks him to forgive her for her previous coldness and disregard.

Pip stands up and is "bending over her"- as if he is inviting her to kiss him- but she says that they will "continue friends apart".

Pip leaves the site of Satis House for the last time, holding Estella's hand. **The mists are rising, as they were when he left the village for London; then, he had hopes and expectations which turned out to be false.**

Now, amidst similarly rising mists, the novel ends with Pip's cryptic and ambiguous comment, "I saw no shadow of another parting from her".

What does this mean?

It could mean that he foresees no further parting, but there was one- that, just as his hopes of life away from the forge were covered in the mists of illusion and deception, his instinct here is again quite wrong.

Or it could mean that he did not foresee another parting from Estella because there was to be no such parting; that, humbled and forgiven as they both are, they are now ready and able to make the same happy ending for themselves that Joe and Biddy, Herbert and Clara, and Wemmick and Miss Skiffins have made. **In this case, they, too, achieve lasting happiness and contentment in the end**, but only once the influence and "parentage" of Magwitch and Miss Havisham are over and done with. At last, the two children have grown up, and, in growing up, they have become adults who can have a grown up relationship.

Critics who persist in the view that Pip is morally flawed and deserves to be punished will prefer the first interpretation. I prefer the second, on the grounds that **Pip and Estella** have both suffered enough, and **have arrived at true self-knowledge. Other people have imposed great expectations on them, and have tried to turn them away from and against their nature**. As Estella says here, they did not put up much "determined resistance". What they have learned is that money cannot guarantee happiness, or control, or satisfaction- lessons which Magwitch and Miss Havisham had not learned. The abuse of the power of money can make people miserable- or lead them into criminal activity, with fatal consequences. The Colonel and Compeyson were both forgers of money.

What matters is, as Joe would put it, what degree of goodness you have in your "hart". Joe tends to be sentimental and less resourceful than he should- he excuses bad behaviour and cowardice in himself and in others. But he was right, when he observed, in chapter 27, that **"life is made of ever so many partings welded together…….Divisions……must be met as they come".**

Just as Joe knows that he is "wrong out of the forge", **Estella is wrong in Satis House, Pip is wrong in London**, and Wopsle is wrong in the theatre. **Great expectations**- both our own, and others'- lead us away from our natural place, and so they **get in the way of**, rather than offer a short cut to, **happiness.** But do they do so for ever; or can we recover from them, to lead balanced and successful lives, as **survivors of great expectations**?

Summary- chapters 57-59

Pip's illness saves him from being taken to a debtor's prison. Joe pays the debt on his behalf, and nurses him back to health. Even the village postman is married. Miss Havisham, influenced by Pip, has left £4000 to Matthew Pocket in a late revision of her Will. Orlick is in prison, not for the murder of Mrs Joe, but for breaking into Pumblechook's house. Joe is unaware of Pip's loss of his wealth, though he is aware that his benefactor is dead; he assumes that Pip will continue in his London way of life, and that, while they share memories of the past and an unbreakable loyalty to each other, their futures lie on different paths.

Because Joe's sense of inferiority makes him leave, unannounced, as soon as Pip's health is better, Dickens can invent, for Pip, a pretext to return to the forge- in order to propose to Biddy. Pip's sense that this is a true homecoming for him meets with the surprise that the school (where Biddy teaches) is closed; that Joe's forge is closed; and that Biddy has married Joe on this very day.

The homecoming becomes another parting. Pip now has no reason to refuse the job Herbert offered him, and he describes himself to Joe and Biddy as "thankless......ungenerous and unjust". They bear no grudge towards him.

Eleven years later, there is another small boy called Pip- Joe and Biddy's son. Biddy knows, intuitively, that Pip cannot, himself, marry or settle until he has completely set aside his infatuation with Estella. He knows that Drummle had died two years previously, but he does not know whether Estella has since remarried.

The final scene reunites Pip and Estella. She is "greatly changed", and the beauty which had so blinded the young Pip has faded. Estella concedes that she had not valued Pip, and had "thrown (him) away". Her own suffering has made her conscious of the value of friendship, but it is unclear whether she is now capable of love. Pip recalls telling Magwitch that he loved Estella; it seems that she is still not yet able to have the relationship with him which he wants.

Dickens leaves the question of what happens next deliberately ambiguous.
Pip's partings- from the village (twice), from Magwitch, from Joe, and from Estella- have always been unsatisfactory. As Joe had said in Chapter 27, "life is made of ever so many partings welded together.....divisions....must be met as they come". In terms of Dickens' biography, Pip's romantic obsession with Estella and his high-handed treatment of Biddy are expressions of his own feelings (including guilt) about his wife

Kate and for Ellen Ternan. In terms of the meaning of the narrative, the end of the novel tells us that what seems like good fortune may turn out to be anything but that, and that we need to address the flaws in our own character, first, if we are to make intimate relationships, because, otherwise, our relationships will be as damaged as we are ourselves.

Cast List and Chapter Locations- Book Three

Use this handy checklist to save time and speed your revision. In particular, if you want to spend a session studying one particular character, use this list to find when – and the location where - they appear.

Chapter 40 Pip and Magwitch, at home; Pip and Jaggers, at Jaggers' office

Chapter 41 Pip and Herbert at home; Magwitch returns for breakfast

Chapter 42 Pip and Herbert hear Magwitch's story, following from the previous chapter

Chapter 43 Pip returns to see Estella and Miss Havisham; first, he stops at the Blue Boar, where he meets Drummle

Chapter 44 Pip, Estella and Miss Havisham, at Satis House

Chapter 45 Pip overnight at the Hummums Hotel; Pip, Wemmick and the aged P, at Wemmick's

Chapter 46 Pip, Herbert, Magwitch, Clara Barley and her father at Mrs Whimple's; Pip and Herbert at home

Chapter 47 Pip at the theatre to see Wopsle, who sees Compeyson in the audience

Chapter 48 Jaggers, Pip and Wemmick, at Little Britain and at Jaggers' house in Gerrard St

Chapter 49 Pip and Miss Havisham at Satis House; she is seriously injured in the fire

Chapter 50 Pip and Herbert, at home

Chapter 51 Pip, Jaggers and Wemmick at Little Britain

Chapter 52 Pip and Herbert, at home, plan the escape down river; Pip has to travel to the marshes, summoned by an anonymous letter to go to the sluice-house for "information about his uncle"

Chapter 53 Pip and Orlick at the sluice-house; Pip rescued by Herbert, Startop and Trabb's boy; back home, ready to move Magwitch down the Thames

Chapter 54 Pip, Herbert, Startop and Magwitch row down the Thames; stay overnight at a waterside pub; Magwitch is arrested just as they are about to escape; Compeyson drowns; Pip returns to London on the police boat, with the injured and condemned Magwitch

Chapter 55 Pip and Herbert at home; Pip at Wemmick's wedding

Chapter 56 Magwitch's trial and sentencing; his death in hospital (all with Pip)

Chapter 57 Joe nurses Pip through his illness, in London

Chapter 58 Pip and Pumblechook at the Blue Boar; Pip with Joe and Biddy at their house

Chapter 59 Pip revisits Joe and Biddy, 11 years later; and meets Estella at the site of Satis House

Now that we have looked Chapter by Chapter, we can look at the mechanics of the novel as a whole.

Firstly, **What does the novel "meantersay" (to borrow a phrase from Joe)?**

Dickens set himself the task, in this novel, of **combining the tragic and the comic**, partly because he had been accused of lacking humour in his more recent writing. He also needed to entertain his contemporary readers, and unfold the story at a leisurely pace, because of the way the novel was published- in instalments.

The plot of "Great Expectations" is satisfying for the reader, because **every puzzle or mystery is resolved, apart from the ambivalent ending, which leaves open the question of where Pip and Estella go from here**. Pip's journey from poverty to wealth and back again, and his parallel journey from childhood to adulthood, both reach their natural conclusion. There are echoes, too, of the parable of the Prodigal Son- Pip has gone into the world with the inheritance he had from Magwitch (though he only spends a small part of it); he has returned, penniless, and repentant, to commit himself, as an adult, to a form of apprenticeship (as Herbert's clerk, rather than Joe's apprentice) and he no longer scorns semi-skilled work as dull or beneath his dignity.

Herbert, Wemmick and Joe are all happily married. Magwitch, Miss Havisham, Drummle and Mrs Joe are dead. Estella, like Pip, has learned to live with herself and has unlearned the damaging and naive attitudes of her youth.

Secondly, **What does the title of the novel- "Great Expectations"- refer to?**

On one level, it draws our attention to **the impact of having money, or not having it**. As Pip says, ruefully, in Chapter 58, of the way he is treated at the Blue Boar-

"Whereas the Boar had cultivated my good opinion with warm assiduity when I was coming into property, the Boar was exceedingly cool on the subject now that I was going out of property."

Matthew Pocket's servants are corrupt and corrupting and careless; so are Pip's laundress, whom Joe dismisses, Orlick, and Pip's manservant "the Avenger". Pip's journey into the adult world starts with the news Jaggers brings him that he now has, through his secret benefactor, great expectations, and must be educated sufficiently well to take the place in society of a gentleman. **Pip, too, has great expectations, not because he longs for material comfort, but of being accepted as the young man whom Estella is expected to marry**. He expects that his entrée into the world away from his village on the marshes will secure a romantic life in which he lives happily ever after.

Miss Havisham has great expectations of Estella. (But, ultimately, she refuses to conform).

Magwitch has great expectations of Pip. (But his fortune dies with him).

Wopsle has great expectations of his career in the theatre. (But he is ridiculous on the stage).

Miss Havisham's grasping relatives- Camilla, Georgina, and Sarah Pocket- are frustrated in their expectations, as Miss Havisham leaves them what they deserve- almost nothing.

Orlick and Compeyson have great expectations of avenging themselves on Pip and Magwitch; they fail too.

In every case, **where there are great expectations, there is great unhappiness, frustration, and, ultimately, failure**.

On the other hand, **where characters have no great expectations**- Joe and Biddy, Herbert and Clara, Matthew Pocket, Wemmick and the Aged P, even Jaggers, and, above all, Magwitch- where they have settled at a level they accept, **so that their lives are not full of strain and aspiration, they find satisfaction and contentment. Pip, too, has reached this point when the novel ends.**

This raises a major question- <u>**is Dickens trying to say that ambition and aspiration are bad**</u>?

Is he a reactionary social conservative who believes that we all have a set place in the hierarchy of society, and that, as Biddy says of Joe's life at the forge, it may be a mistake to "let any one take him out of a place that he is competent to fill, and fills well and with respect"?. **Displacement**- particularly the displacement of Pip, from the village to London- **seems not to work**. Joe knows that London is an alien place; Wopsle cannot adjust to it, and, for Pip, it never feels like home. Estella's "finishing" in France and at Richmond leave her bored and jaded. Wemmick has his Walworth sentiments and his very different personality or identity at work in Little Britain. On the other hand, Drummle and Orlick are brutes wherever they go; and Magwitch can adapt to any habitat. Pip is uprooted suddenly (like Hamlet's ghost) and he wanders in a kind of Purgatory, removed from his village, but unable to settle in London.

Dickens reinforces the lack of a satisfactory identity, of a sense of completeness, of being fully known (and accepted for who you are), **by his widespread use of partial names for so many of his characters here. What are the Christian names of Jaggers, Miss Havisham, Mrs Joe, Pumblechook , Compeyson, the Aged P, Miss Skiffins, Startop, Wopsle, Pip's servant Pepper, or Trabb's boy? What is Biddy's surname?**

And then there is Pip himself. **Why is Pip called "Pip","Mr Pip", "Handel", and "dear boy"? Is it because he has never yet grown up to the point where other characters will call him "Mr Pirrip"? And is the point of Pip's name (both his Christian name and his surname) that it is palindromic- that it takes him back to where he came from originally?**

Magwitch has aliases- Provis, Mr Campbell, or "Tom, Jack, or Richard"; presumably, his (ex-)wife Molly has an assumed surname. Their identity is hidden in order to protect them from trial and punishment.

I find the idea of some critics that the novel is about Pip's "snobbishness", for which he has to be punished, unhelpful; that is not where the emotional centre of the narrative lies.

Pip feels guilty for helping Magwitch, just as he feels guilty about benefiting from Magwitch's money- not because the favour Pip did him is being repaid a disproportionate number of times over, but **because he feels it is wrong to abet a criminal. Jaggers, on the other hand, abets criminals all the time, including**

Estella's mother; and he seems to be outside the law. Dickens does not choose to inflict any form of punishment on him.

The heart of the story is, rather, about loyalty.

Magwitch and Pip are loyal to each other in a way which cannot be measured. Pip is acutely conscious of his lack of loyalty to Joe and Biddy. But his neglect of them, and Joe's subsequent unease with him, is not the result of snobbishness (despite Trabb's boy and his pantomime chant of "don't know yah"). Trabb, Pumblechook and the management of the Blue Boar treat Pip obsequiously- their attitude to money is at least as much responsible for the distortion of the old loyalties as his is. **Pip and Herbert have a friendship characterised by absolute loyalty. So do Wemmick and his father, and Jaggers and Wemmick**. Compeyson and Orlick are utterly disloyal. Magwitch forces the young Pip to be loyal to him, and Pip stresses, in his childish way, that he has not betrayed him. **Loyalty is a quality it is impossible to put a financial price on, and Magwitch repays it with everything he has, including his own life. Molly's secret guilt forces her to be loyal to Jaggers, but her daughter's loyalty to Miss Havisham becomes conditional when the demands made of her become too great.**

This novel presents **life** as rather like the fight Herbert insists on having with Pip. It **can be painful**, and it often involves people mistaking what is really going on- Herbert seems to think he is winning, when he is losing. The ability to absorb punishment- to take blows, and still smile and maintain your optimism- is a sign of good nature. **There is no problem resilience cannot overcome**.

In the end, the characters Dickens gives us here fall into three groups.

Group One. Those who are resilient (and therefore good) are Pip, Joe, Herbert and Matthew Pocket, Magwitch and Estella.

Group Two. Those who are disloyal (or antisocial) are Orlick, Miss Havisham and her relatives, Compeyson and Mrs Joe- they are violent and/or vengeful.

Group Three – the mixed bag. Jaggers and Wemmick are like London (or "Little Britain") itself- solid, dark, very aware that money makes the world go round, capable of murky behaviour but also capable of softness and occasional, fleeting compassion.

In the end, though money circulates, it eventually has little value. Jaggers' kindness to Estella, and Pip's kindness to Herbert, bring lasting, lifelong benefits far greater than Magwitch's generosity. Generosity can sometimes be frustrated; but the negative behaviour of the second group of characters never succeeds in the end.

Some critics detect a specifically Christian morality at work in the structure of the novel. They argue that it is the tale of Pip's "sin" and redemption through suffering. The problem with this is that, although all of his childhood experience has taught Pip to feel guilty, he has little or nothing to feel guilty about; he is not "naterally wicious" at all, but a small boy growing up in a harsh environment.

When he is removed to London, Pip is socially naïve. Nothing in his life in the village can prepare him for the exploitative behaviour of coachmen, or the servants he employs. Being bullied by Mrs Joe is a training course for being bullied by Miss Havisham.

Cruelty and evil exists both in the village (Orlick) and in the wider world (Compeyson). So does nobility, generosity and loyalty (Biddy and Joe; Wemmick and Herbert). Pip and Estella both have to free themselves from the shackles their (well-meaning?) "parents", Magwitch and Miss Havisham, try to control them with. Pip's money and Estella's emotional coldness are handicaps which bar their way to happiness.

Dickens' own feelings of the need to conform to the expectations of the polite society he lived in, and the need to break away from his wife, may be the key here. His novel dramatizes the tension between what others expect from us- which crushes us, emotionally- and the romantic dreams or expectations we harbour for ourselves.

Perhaps the way in which Pip loses everything material, but finally finds himself, is a metaphor for Dickens' own sense of social entrapment. Pip never transfers his affections away from Estella. Dickens probably envies his character this consistency, because it avoids the emotional turmoil which seems to have been characteristic of Dickens himself.

"Gentlemen" and gentlemen - and how Important is it to be one in "Great Expectations"?

The term "gentleman" originally came into the English language from French; in Chaucer's "The Canterbury Tales" the concept of "gentillesse" is analysed; it means a type of selfless or even self-sacrificing nobility. **The "gentleman" will put his own interests second to the interests of others he is morally responsible for. He will fulfil his obligations, regardless of the inconvenience or disadvantage he suffers as a result.**

This is precisely the way Pip behaves towards Magwitch once he has overcome his initial aversion to the scruffy figure who turns up at his London lodgings in Chapter 39. Protecting Magwitch from the death sentence he has risked, in coming to see the "gentleman" he has made (Pip) is Pip's mission, even after he has decided that he must not benefit from money which he fears may have been generated through criminal activity.

Pip has learned the value of loyalty from Joe, who is a gentleman minus the necessary education. Just as Pip refuses to take possession of Magwitch's "portable property", Joe refused money from both Miss Havisham and Jaggers, because it would have offended his dignity and independence to take it.

Pip's "great expectations" mean that he can buy the clothes, books and jewellery which denote gentlemanliness. But he takes time to grow into those clothes; hence the way Trabb's boy mocks him in the street. Pip sees himself as the romantic knight who will save Satis House and rescue Estella, but he manages to do neither.

It is **Trabb's boy** who **rescues him** from death at the hands of Orlick (with Herbert and Startop). **That experience seems to galvanise Pip into a new maturity; he starts to put right the relationships which have fallen into neglect, and to show the instinct to forgive and to ask for forgiveness which is one of the defining marks of the gentleman. Before long, his care for Magwitch becomes unconnected with his expectations, and it is only when he has arrived at an understanding with Estella which no longer has anything to do with self-interest that Pip has the slightest possibility of the romantic relationship with her which has always been his fixation.**

Herbert sets an example which Pip follows. Despite his own lack of expectations, Herbert helps Pip with London life (and table manners). There is no shred of resentment on his part of the apparent fact that Pip has been preferred to him as a match for Estella.

To see Pip's journey as one of sin and redemption is to adopt the ludicrous Pumblechookian morality which Dickens invites us to laugh at. It is more helpful to the meaning of the novel for us to **see the difference between the empty, external trappings of gentility and the behaviours it requires**.

Estella, bored with the "finishing" in France and at Richmond which will make her the female equivalent of a gentleman, throws herself away on Drummle because she does not wish to inflict pain any more on sensitive boys. Pip's experiences of how people are saved from danger, criminality and criminal conviction (Molly, Estella, and- thanks to Joe paying the bailiff- himself), and of how they are not saved (Magwitch, the Colonel in Chapter 32,) lead him to a proper understanding of **what loyalty is- an unromantic, self-sacrificing concern for the welfare of others, regardless of their wealth or social status.**

Gaining confidence as you answer essay questions and answers

This book has been set out so that you can answer essay questions more easily, simply by referring to the list of characters and locations, to identify which chapters to use. You can then using the notes and analysis on each of those chapters. Why not try this approach out on essay questions you are set in class, or that you want to use to practise during your revision?

I show how the method works below.

Example Essay Question 1

"A major fault of the novel is the fact that Pip idolises Estella, but the reader does not". Explain to what extent you agree with this judgment.

Source material- Chapters 8, 11, 12, 15, 29, 33, 38, 44, 59

Answer

Although Estella features prominently in Pip's story, she is only part of it. She appears in a relatively small number of the 59 chapters, and not at all between chapters 45 and 58.

When Pip first meets her, he thinks she is like a queen, although she (a fellow 8-year-old) treats him haughtily and calls him "boy" (like Pumblechook). She hints that the original owners of Satis House were "easily satisfied"- we come to see that she has no desire to satisfy others, least of all Pip. He rightly identifies her as "very pretty……proud…..insulting"; when he says she is less insulting, on his next visit, she slaps him. Pip has been conditioned to physical violence, as Mrs Joe has "brought him up by hand"- he thinks it is normal for girls and women to behave like this.

Estella makes Pip painfully conscious of his "coarse" background. He imagines her looking in at the forge and laughing at him; she drives his social ambition, which is suddenly realisable, with Magwitch's fortune. Pip imagines that his rags to riches fairytale story will extend to him restoring the light to Satis House and rescuing Estella (Chapter 29). Through his misunderstanding, and his assumption that Miss Havisham has chosen him for preferment (Herbert also assumes this), Pip convinces himself that he and Estella will be married and live happily ever after.

In fact, Miss Havisham has sent her to France as early as Chapter 15. Dickens works hard in Chapter 29 to make us feel that Pip's behaviour, in an adolescent boy, is natural, although it is "against reason.....hope....happiness". The language Pip uses ("enchantment") is the language of the fairy princess with her magic wand. We find the concept of romantic enthralment in the literature of the time- for example, Emily Bronte's "Wuthering Heights" (1847), and in Keats' ballad "La belle dame sans merci", which was written in 1819 and is very much of the time of Pip's adolescence. When Miss Havisham urges Pip to love Estella, in Chapter 29, it sounds "like a curse"- like the destructive, obsessive love of Keats' poem.

By Chapter 33, Pip is beginning to understand that his hopes of Estella are ill-fated; so his understanding does not lag too far behind the reader's. In Chapter 43, his scuffle with Drummle does not hide the fact that he knows he has lost the battle for Estella's hand in marriage; Drummle's pursuit of Estella, or the way she attracts "ugly creatures" to the "candle" of her beauty, had come to the surface in chapter 38 .

In Chapters 8 and 12, Pip hears, or half hears, Miss Havisham telling Estella to "break their hearts". Once we know that Estella is her adopted daughter, and that Miss Havisham has controlled her so closely from her infancy (when her mother gave her up to Jaggers) we have rather more sympathy for Estella, because we understand the source of her behaviour.

As readers, we accept at face value Estella's warning or explanation to Pip that she has "no softness.....sympathy....sentiment"- in effect, no heart or "tenderness". Pip does not accept it because he believes that it is his destiny to be with Estella. Eventually, in Chapter 44, Pip confesses his love to Estella, and she continues knitting, because she cannot "comprehend" the "sentiments" he is expressing. She says that, while her lack of feeling may be unnatural, "it is in the nature formed within me".

Estella's blushing delight and excitement at Pip's fistfight with Herbert in Chapter 11 foreshadows the violence she suffers in her marriage to the brutal Drummle. When they meet in the final chapter, she describes herself as "bent and broken"- but her own experience, and the death of Miss Havisham, has turned her into a different person; she has found her identity, and, with it, an understanding of Pip's "worth". Estella describes herself as "greatly changed"- rather like Rochester in Charlotte Bronte's "Jane Eyre", the hero's love object here has gained wisdom through suffering, and her physical pride and beauty has been stripped away.

There is no fairy tale ending in which the boy, having met the girl and lost the girl, lives happily ever after with her. Dickens leaves us to complete the tale in that way if we so wish (Pip's great expectations of Estella would then finally be achieved), but readers who prefer a permanent separation can infer that too.

As he narrates his own biography to us, Pip applies the wisdom of hindsight to his feelings about Estella all those years ago. We understand that he tells the tale through a filter of self-knowledge; and Dickens goes to great lengths to tie the attraction of Estella to Pip's feelings of dissatisfaction with his poor and low origins.

Magwitch's intended kindness to Pip leads to complications which are anything but happy. Estella, like Pip, is a victim- of her own mother and of her stepmother, Miss Havisham. Jaggers and Molly meant to save Estella but they could not have known how damaging Miss Havisham's obsessions would be. In this context, Estella becomes more sympathetic to us, and Pip's delusions become forgivable and excusable too.

The relationship between Pip and Estella is pivotal to Pip's growing up. It starts with him idolising her, and us resenting her high-handedness and snobbery towards him. It ends with us understanding why she had behaved in that way. Pip stops idolising her in the last third of the novel, and she stops being Miss Havisham's puppet, or ice princess, and grows into a humbler and wiser adult. Her journey of development happens off-stage, but it is quite like Pip's own escape from the dark shadows and influences of the Magwitch family's secrets. In the end, we sympathise with Pip, and we sympathise with Estella, too.   (960 words)

Example Essay Question 2

"The character of Miss Havisham may belong in a fairy tale, but it has no place in a novel which claims to depict characters realistically". Explain how far you agree with this view, and why.

Source material- Chapters 8, 11, 12, 13, 19, 29, 38, 44 and 49

We know that Dickens was fascinated by the (imagined) behaviour and motivation of female recluses. There is a supposed model for Miss Havisham- a so-called "white woman" who could be seen on Oxford Street wearing a wedding dress, and was driven mad by her rejection by a wealthy Quaker she had hoped to marry. Dickens had published an article about her in 1853.

There are elements of the fairy tale "wicked witch" in the character of Miss Havisham, but she is more complex than that. Dickens prepares the way for her lingering death after the fire at Satis House by describing her, in earlier chapters, as zombie-like. Estella's marriage to Drummle leaves her with no victims to exploit and no reason to continue living.

Miss Havisham is a study in what goes wrong when you give in to obsession. The descriptions of Satis House, with its barred windows, locked door, overgrown garden, stopped clocks, and lack of fresh air and daylight, reflect the closed, isolated and diseased state of its owner's mind.

Being jilted at the altar is, no doubt, traumatic, but it does not justify going over to the dark side. Miss Havisham is bad; not as bad as the murderous Orlick (whom she employs as her gatekeeper) but bad enough for even the arch-villain Compeyson to dupe and abandon her.

Victorian readers had a taste for melodrama, and fires were a popular feature in novels. Novelists used them to purify their heroes' antagonists (Charlotte Bronte's"Jane Eyre", Elizabeth Barrett Browning's "Aurora Leigh"), and Miss Havisham survives the fire long enough to ask for forgiveness in a speech pattern which echoes that of the dying Mrs Joe (Chapters 49, 35). She has already begged Pip to forgive her for the emotional cruelty she has inflicted on him, as she sought to avenge Compeyson's cruelty to her on all men, through Estella.

While Magwitch seeks to repay (Pip's) kindness with magnified kindness (to Pip), Miss Havisham seeks to repay Compeyson's cruelty with magnified cruelty to all men; this is disproportionate, and it throws away Estella's finer feelings too. She had not asked Estella to forgive her, when they argued, in Chapter 38; there, in a scene with strong echoes of Shakespeare's "King Lear", Miss Havisham (Queen Lear, if there were such a character) accuses Estella (Cordelia) of a lack of love, or ingratitude ("Ingratitoode" is also what Pumblechook accuses Pip of), and Estella argues back that she is the product or creature of her maker's will. Here, Miss Havisham is not so much the wicked witch of the fairy tale as the experimental scientist who seeks to modify nature or genetic inheritance.

Dickens presents his characters in "Great Expectations" in a range of ways. Jaggers, Magwitch and Joe are very lifelike, because they have mannerisms and body language which is personal to them. Wemmick is different- he keeps the safe key on a piece of string around his neck, but otherwise has no personal movements; instead, he is "wooden" and his mouth is like a "post office". Orlick and Mrs Joe are defined by the violence of their behaviour, rather than by what they say. Drummle has a distinctive way of speaking, as do Camilla and Herbert. Estella and Pip are the most rounded and fully explored characters. Miss Havisham has a distinctive place, both in the detail Dickens describes her with, and in the extent to which she is allowed to speak for herself.

In Chapter 8, Dickens introduces us to her as a "skeleton in the ashes of a rich dress", and as "corpse-like", dressed in a wedding outfit which, counter-intuitively, has the character of "grave-clothes…the long veil so like a shroud": a mummified creature which might "fall to powder" if touched. The wind which blows round Satis House is like her- cold, shrill and howling. Her physical appearance is a reflection of her psychological condition- she has "dropped, body and soul….under the weight of a crushing blow". Much of her behaviour is obsessive and ritualistic- the insistence on card games, or on Pip wheeling her round the room, wandering the corridors in the middle of the night, or holding jewels against Estella's skin- in the manner of a ghost or a zombie.

The imagery has changed when she next appears, in Chapter 11- she looks like a witch, and has " a withered hand" (hands are always significant- Jaggers', Molly's, Estella's especially)- but she still talks, on her birthday, about how, when she dies, she will be laid out on the table here. There are hints of cannibalism- her grasping relatives will "feast" on her, while she has been "gnawed" by teeth sharper than mice's teeth (by cruelty and betrayal). In Chapter 29, she has "withered arms….a clenched hand", and she kisses Estella's hand with a "ravenous intensity"; she clutches it in Chapter 38. When she realises how badly she has treated Pip, she constantly holds "her hand to her heart".

Miss Havisham's eyes are a significant component of her character- "sunken….watchful….brooding" in Chapter 8, "weird" in Chapter 19, and "ghastly" in

Chapter 44, when she realises her own cruelty. In Chapter 49, she uses the image of vision to describe her own life as "blind".

At other times, her mind seems clear, and she speaks and behaves in a coherent way- when she meets Joe in Chapter 13.

As we come closer to her exit from the narrative, Miss Havisham goes through a mental decline which mirrors her physical collapse- she is "mumbling.... trembling....wasting" in Chapter 38, and wailing a "low cry" as she wanders at night.

Even over a distance of 150 years, Miss Havisham is an authentic representation of acute mental distress, if not mental illness. The mind of a fairy tale character is never of interest; but Miss Havisham's habitat reflects her decay and decline.

Rather like Mrs Joe, she is a controlling woman who would describe herself as strong and benevolent, but whom others would describe as bullying and oppressive. Her mission is misguided but her thoroughness and determination in pursuing it is unstoppable, although it leads to her own destruction (in the fire). Pip forgives her for her treatment of him; like him, she uses her money to help Herbert, and that unselfish generosity is a redemptive act.

Miss Havisham belongs in a novel because her behaviour and motivation raise a moral issue; how far is vengeance justified? Betrayed by Compeyson, she takes revenge on all men, through Estella, whom she has trained to break the hearts of all men. Society, betrayed by criminals, takes indiscriminate and disproportionate vengeance on them (while sparing the murderer Orlick). Miss Havisham has expectations of Estella which her stepdaughter finally rejects. Dickens is using her to prove the point that public revenge, on a grand scale, for a private transgression, is wrong. Miss Havisham's attitude to crime and punishment is unhealthy, the product of a sick mind. And the justice system Dickens gives us in "Great Expectations" is a similarly misguided response of a sick, though collective, mind.

While Miss Havisham superficially resembles a character from a fairy tale- she starts as the fairy godmother but turns out to be the wicked witch- she is one of the several characters whose great expectations eventually turn out badly. In her own limited way, she learns where she has gone too far, from Estella's rejection of her values; she learns that emotional frigidity is wrong, and warmth is right, just as Pip learns that loyalty is right.   (1250 words)

How to succeed in your exam - what you need to know

If you are studying "Great Expectations" for AQA or OCR or WJEC, the appropriate websites are an important place to look.

Each exam board has a website where you can see the questions set in previous years, become familiar with, and understand, how answers are marked, and read the examiners' reports.

Those reports highlight the strengths and weaknesses of each year's scripts. From them, we can make a list of positive and negative points; more of that in a moment.

At GCSE, The AQA exam will print a passage and ask you to use it to explain and analyse *how* a character (Pip, Estella, Joe) or a group of characters (Pip's friends, the female characters,) is presented; or *how* some aspect of life is shown to us (grief, greed, exploitation, dreams).

A question of this type is designed to see whether you can select the important details from a short passage and show how they help to construct the larger meaning in the novel. The emphasis is *on what we are shown.* This tests our understanding of Dickens' broader values and the moral issues (crime and punishment, social class, fairness, discrimination, envy) he wants us to think about.

Try to develop a clear understanding of the role of each character, by asking yourself what would be missing from the novel if that character were not there?

OCR questions have tended to be rather different. They often ask us to explain and analyse *how and why we respond* emotionally to a particular episode; in other words, how conscious we are of what Dickens does with language. The issue "how does he do this" asks us to explain what lies behind the lines, not just what the passage says.

Sensible analysis of foreshadowing and symbolism will help you here. Look, too, for the words and phrases which have the most resonance, and lead us to be involved with the action emotionally (we sympathise with the weak).

The key skills here are showing that we can analyse Dickens' purpose, and that we can explain how and why we, as readers, respond as we do. What is he putting into our minds, and why?

In the OCR exam, you will have a choice; a passage-based question, which will be about Dickens' language and methods, or a novel-wide question which asks you to show how well you understand the themes of the narrative as a whole.

Examiners' reports stress that marks are given for commenting on what is in the passage- so we have to have *evidence* for our view. This means that there is a rule you should follow- if it isn't in the novel, leave it out!! Good evidence will be backed up with quotations. It is often enough to quote a short phrase, or even a single word, to prove your point. You will have the book with you – the skill is in knowing it well enough to be able to find the quotes you want quickly.

The best answers will also avoid over-interpreting detail, but will start by observing details, will have sound and interesting things to say about why Dickens has chosen them, and may draw from that some wider conclusions about the context in which he was writing. Here you might take the example of how, in Dickens' age, characters approaching death sought to redeem themselves from sin, in keeping with the moral, Christian views of the time.

Markers are always interested in your personal response (provided it's sensible, and explained)- so, for example, don't be afraid to analyse where and why you feel uncomfortable with what a character says or how they say it. A good example would be where Pip considers marrying Biddy, but thinks only of what the match would offer him, not her.

More broadly, it is important to avoid repetition, because it suggests you have too little to say. What is important is your focus on the question. Identify key words in the question, and don't answer some other question you would have preferred to find! If you are answering a question about a set passage, write about that passage- refer to other episodes for evidence to prove your points, but keep your focus firmly on the passage in front of you.

You will be much less likely to lose marks for irrelevant material if you PLAN your answer carefully and thoroughly before you write it.

There is always a strong temptation to start writing straight away, in a timed exam- especially if you see people around you doing just that. But the exam allows time to plan, and it is almost impossible to get a really good mark without a really good plan.

If you have read the book, and taken a little time to think about what it means to say to us, you will have plenty of good material.

The test in the exam is, then, to choose the right material, put it into an effective structure, and use your points to construct an argument, which you support by reference to the text.

Seven or eight points are likely to be enough, because you will then need to develop them, and show why they are important.

You should develop each of your points in one paragraph. Try to use fairly short sentences. When you have finished, go on to your next point. Then write a summary/concluding paragraph to say which point is most important, and why.

Before you start writing your answer, put your points in order of importance, and write about them in that order, with the most important first. Keep going. If you run out of time for that question, you must move on to the next one; it matters less to have left out your least important point than your most important one.

Don't try to write too much, but constantly check that *what you are writing is relevant to the question.*

And before you take the exam, ask your teacher to explain again how the mark scheme works. Then you will have at the front of your mind your understanding of what you will be given marks for, and what you won't.

Especially if you are to take your exam in summer 2018 and 2019, I wish you every success.

Gavin Smithers is a private tutor, covering Broadway, Chipping Campden and the north Cotswolds. He has an English degree from Oxford University and a passion for helping others to discover the joy and satisfaction of great literature.

Gavin's Guides are short books packed with insight. Their key aim is to help you raise your grade! Ask for more information at grnsmithers@hotmail.co.uk

Printed in Great Britain
by Amazon